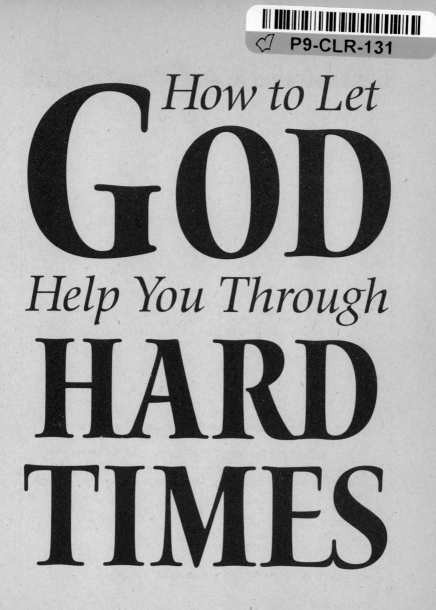

How to Let

GOD

Help You Through

HARD
TIMES

Publications International, Ltd.

P9-CLR-131

Cover credits: **Ken Graham/Tony Stone Images** (background).

Copyright © 2001 Publications International, Ltd. All rights reserved. This book may not be reproduced or quoted in whole or in part by any means whatsoever without written permission from:

Louis Weber, CEO
Publications International, Ltd.
7373 North Cicero Avenue
Lincolnwood, Illinois 60712

Permission is never granted for commercial purposes.

Manufactured in U.S.A.

8 7 6 5 4 3 2 1

ISBN: 0-7853-4440-3

CONTENTS

INTRODUCTION

IN THE COURSE of every life, there will be times of tragedy, sorrow, fear, and confusion. Times when there appears to be no light at the end of the tunnel and happiness is but a wisp on the wind floating farther from our grasp. We feel lost and alone, unable to regain our footing.

It is then that we ask, "Why, God? Why did this happen to me? How will I get through this? Will I ever be happy again?" In our longing to understand, we meet a moment of defeat when we simply cannot take another step forward without help from something greater than ourselves.

This is the moment we stop trying to fix things, control things, and make things happen, and we turn it over to God. For God has the perfect blueprint for our lives. We surrender, and that's when his work begins.

In these moments come gifts of hope and clarity. Something within us stirs back to life, and our broken hearts and shattered spirits sense that healing is afoot. We begin to feel the support of a loving God who wants us to know joy again and who wants us to move through that despair and come out stronger, wiser, and kinder.

We recognize what we've always known but somehow have forgotten in our times of suffering: that we are never really alone and lost; that a power far grander than we could ever imagine is always by our side, guiding us and urging us onward; and that we are always right where we need to be in our path to spiritual growth.

In these moments, God's grace comes pouring down upon us like sweet and nourishing rain. What was once dry and dead is brought back to life; what was weak is made strong. Pain and anguish give way to acceptance and understanding, and anger is transformed into forgiveness. We test our once-broken wings to find they are whole again, and we take flight.

In these moments, when we ask God to help us through hard times, the power of love is made evident, for there is no power like it.

The members of the first-century church in Philippi suffered severe persecution because of their faith in Jesus Christ, but a letter came to them from a dear old friend, who encouraged them to remain faithful to God. The apostle Paul wrote to them:

> Rejoice in the Lord always; again I will say, Rejoice. Let your gentleness be known to everyone. The Lord is near. Do not worry about anything, but in everything by prayer and supplication with thanksgiving let your requests be made known to God. And the peace of God, which surpasses all understanding, will guard your hearts and your minds in Christ Jesus (Phil 4:4-7).

Just as God brought joy and peace to the believers in Philippi nearly two thousand years ago and to the people in this book, he can bring joy and peace to you today.

CHAPTER 1

WHEN DISASTER STRIKES

D ISASTER CAN STRIKE at any time without warning to anyone anywhere. Our lives can change dramatically in one unexpected moment, but in those worst times of our lives, we can lean on family, friends, and even strangers who reach out to us. Yet, even more importantly, we can turn to God, who is always there for us during our darkest hours. He will never fail us, never let us down, and never turn away from us when we cry out to him.

The people in this chapter have faced devastating calamities, and their insights are helpful to anyone who is struggling with the "whys" of a disaster, for in their own way each points to God's presence as a place of refuge.

Curled Up in a Closet

The wind hurled rain against my sliding glass door, and I thought it might smash the glass at any moment. Meanwhile, I watched the dark clouds race across the sky. As the surrounding trees shook violently, I worried that they'd snap off and fly against my trembling windows. When I stepped outside, I heard police officers with their bullhorns call out warnings from their patrol cars.

I will say of the Lord, "He is my refuge and my fortress, my God; in whom I trust."

PSALM 91:2 NIV

I'd been glued to my portable radio once the power failed across the city. According to the broadcaster, the entire mid-section of the country was under siege. Storm after storm tore across 13 states, producing terrible tornadoes, more than ever before in such a brief time. Word had gradually filtered through, telling of entire communities destroyed, towns leveled, property severely damaged, and lives lost. Reports were still sketchy. With power down and storm damage extensive, news came slowly, and rumors spread quickly. It was hard to believe such frightening things were occurring all around us.

I'd never been in a tornado nor seen anything like this before. Fear gripped my heart, and I kept silent beside the radio, listening for news and praying that none of the series of powerful tornadoes would suddenly plow through our city. Through that endless, sleepless night, I fought panic. What would I do if a tornado headed my way? Where would I go? My apartment had never felt so flimsy and fragile. On the third floor with most of one wall made of the sliding glass door, my apartment seemed the worst place in the world to be. But where else could I go? I had no car and no way of getting anywhere else. The entire city was blacked out and at a standstill.

I suspected the only people out on the streets tonight would be dangerous to encounter. So, where could I go? What could I do? I'd asked my neighbors what they were planning to do, but nobody had a good answer. Some claimed huddling inside the bathtub would be safest. Others headed for the lowest floors, staying in friends' apartments. One planned to slide under the bed. Another built a cocoon of mattresses and blankets for protection.

I recalled news footage seen over the years of tornado damage. There weren't many safe places to go, as best I could remember. I'd

> *For thou hast been a strength to the poor, a strength to the needy in his distress, a refuge from the storm.*
>
> ISAIAH 25:4 KJV

seen footage of flattened houses, cars tossed into trees, and whole blocks of buildings gone. People could survive incredibly powerful tornadoes by rushing to storm shelters underground, but I didn't have one. No storm shelter. No basement. No safe place at all.

While listening to sirens scream all across the city, I dove for my large, walk-in closet, pressed myself against an inside wall and prayed with all my strength. Curled up tight, knees against my chest, head down, I listened intently, remembering people say a tornado sounded like a freight train bearing down on you or like a helicopter landing on your roof.

Curled up in that closet during one of the worst nights of my life, I waited, listened, and prayed. Every now and then, I crept out to peer through my window at the menacing sky or slipped outside to check again with neighbors to see if they'd heard anything new. I kept my radio close and carried my flashlight with me.

In that endless 24 hours on April 3 and 4, 1974, more than 100 tornadoes tore across the 13 states, leaving a path of death and destruction behind. None of us would ever forget this night, filled with fear and tension. We never knew where a twister would strike next or if we'd come through safely amid the sirens, warnings, and dreadful news reports. It was a nightmare for everyone who survived.

Through it all there was no truly safe place, no refuge, except in God, and while I prayed that night, I felt His presence watching over us all.

HE WALKS BESIDE ME

Through the darkest days, God walks beside me and will never leave me. His presence comforts me and gives me the courage to keep going no matter what my circumstances are.

Why tornadoes, Lord? Why typhoons or fires? Why floods or earthquakes? Why devastating accidents, Lord? It's so hard to understand. Perhaps there is no way to find any sense in overwhelming circumstances. Perhaps it's about trusting in you, God, no matter what comes and leaving it in your hands, where it belongs because, in fact, you do really love us and care about us and will make things work out for us.

Sweet are the uses of adversity,
Which like the toad, ugly and venomous,
Wears yet a precious jewel in his head…

WILLIAM SHAKESPEARE, *AS YOU LIKE IT*

By Candlelight

While struggles rage, we cling together by candle-light, drawing courage from one another until the dawn comes again. It is then that God will bring us a happier day.

The raging storm may round us beat,
A shelter in the time of storm;
We'll never leave our safe retreat,
A shelter in the time of storm.

Oh, Jesus is a Rock in a weary land,
A weary land, a weary land;
Oh, Jesus is a rock in a weary land,
A shelter in the time of storm.

VERNON J. CHARLESWORTH, "A Shelter in the Time of Storm"

The Right Place to Be

After the storm, they cautiously push open their closet door and creep from their hiding place. How bad is it? They see destruction everywhere.

Nothing left untouched, except for one safe spot—the closet in which the whole family crouched, pressed tight together, frightened, holding one another, praying. One thing remains, upright and safe—their hiding place in time of trouble, their sanctuary, the right place to be.

At disappointment and losses which are the effect of Providential acts, I never repine; because I am sure the allwise Disposer of events knows better than we do what is best for us, or what we deserve.

GEORGE WASHINGTON

A SAFE PLACE

So many terrors and troubles confront us, so many dangers and calamities. Is anyone ever completely safe? Only when we trust God, do we know peace and assurance in the shelter of his care.

To all survivors I have one bit of encouragement, for I know after every disaster there is an aftermath. Long after the headlines are history, the hurt and healing continue. The few others who have known similar circumstances can understand. Let them help.... And most of all God offers strength beyond all possible comprehension. The One who saved me from the tragedy of my life and brought me through the aftermath makes me supremely grateful that I am alive.

SANDY PURL, AM I ALIVE?

O God, our help in ages past,
Our hope for years to come,
Our shelter from the stormy blast,
And our eternal home!

ISAAC WATTS, "O GOD, OUR HELP IN AGES PAST"

EARTHQUAKE CHRISTIANS

In the early morning darkness of December 1811, along the Mississippi River, suddenly the ground rumbled and shook. Settlers in their cabins along the frontier stumbled across jolting floors to tumble outside into a night gone crazy. Animals milled around in distress. Families fell to the ground as their homes broke apart.

Eyewitnesses described a sound like thunder from beneath their feet. Many caught a whiff of noxious fumes, a smell like sulfur, and feared the very gates of hell had split wide. The ground cracked open. The nearby river churned and seethed. Banks collapsed into the water. Trees fell in masses. In the darkness and confusion many thought it was the end of the world.

> *When the earth and all its people quake, it is I who hold its pillars firm.*
> PSALM 75:3 NIV

Some told of the ground rising in waves as if turned to water, and the waves just kept coming and coming. And, as if this terrible earthquake wasn't enough, the ground kept right on shuddering and trembling day after day, month after month. The homes that stood through that first jolt would give way under additional powerful shocks days and months later, as shocks rocked the entire middle of the United States.

So tremendous were the quakes that hundreds of miles away on the East Coast in New York, Washington, D.C., and Maryland, church bells rang, beds shook, pavements cracked, and residents felt some of the fear that affected the settlers' hearts along the Mississippi River in an area that is known today as the New Madrid Seismic Zone.

Over the weeks, the Mississippi River was reported to have flowed backward and form sudden rapids, a huge lake formed in Tennessee, islands in the river vanished, whole forests were flattened, and geysers shot up steam and mud. Hysterical survivors told of the ground cracking open and shut like the jaws of a fierce beast. The river itself changed course drastically, forming new twists and turns, flowing where once homes had stood. River traffic halted. Nobody knew how many boats capsized and were lost. Nobody had an accurate count of how many river travelers were stricken by the quake-agitated river. Nobody even knew how much damage the incredible quakes caused.

For those who lived through it all, there would never be anything like it again. One scientist kept count of tremors over only a few months during the worst of it, and noted some 1,200 shocks of various strengths where he lived in Louisville, Kentucky.

I have set the Lord always before me. Because he is at my right hand, I will not be shaken.

PSALM 16:8 NIV

People abandoned their homes, fleeing from the shaking ground. Some communities ceased to exist by the end of the quakes. Many individuals found their way to churches, believing they faced the end of the world. By the hundreds they came to church and to God, seeking solace and safety. So many massed to those early churches that they were named "Earthquake Christians."

Yet in such a terrible and devastating time, where else could they go except to God? They could not trust the very earth beneath their feet, which rocked them like boats on a rough sea. In their frantic time of horror and need, they rushed to the Lord and his protection and found comfort there. For through all recorded time it's been so, that in dire need, in the worst moments, we turn to God.

Surely there is a future, and your hope will not be cut off.

PROVERBS 23:18

Dear God, please be with this family. I see their faces in a newspaper clipping, and I'm moved by their hurt and their loss. I'll never meet them. I'll never know what they suffered. Though they are strangers to me, they are not strangers to you. Get them through this bad time. Keep them safe and well and close to you. Amen.

A Message to Loved Ones

Amid scattered debris, broken walls and shattered floors, concrete steps lead up to a house no longer there. Crushed chairs and sofas litter the property. Papers flutter in a light breeze.

Spray painted on a propped-up door, a message left behind for family and friends tells it all.

"WE'RE OK. WE'RE AT THE SHELTER."

Faith or Fear

Beneath our feet the earth trembles. No solid ground beneath us. Will our hearts tremble, too? Or will we walk with faith?

Don't demand explanations. Don't lean on your ability to understand. Don't turn loose of your faith. But do choose to trust Him, by the exercise of the will He has placed within you.

James Dobson, When God Doesn't Make Sense

The Bell Tolls for Me

Disaster can strike anyone, anywhere—no one is immune. May we never turn from another's pain. Someday it could be our own.

God whispers to us in our pleasures, speaks in our conscience, but shouts in our pains: it is His megaphone to rouse a deaf world.

C. S. Lewis, *The Problem of Pain*

Everything's Gone

She picks at the bits and pieces of her life amid sodden, fire-scorched debris. She looks up and says, "Everything's gone." Then she smiles in her sorrow, and says, "But we're all safe, thank God."

The call of God involves earthly suffering because through it we may magnify His power to keep us and demonstrate His grace in our weakness.

Earthly suffering, bravely borne, shows powerfully the reality of the living God.

STUART BRISCOE, *WHEN THE GOING GETS TOUGH*

THE VIEW

From a helicopter, the view was staggering. A bomb had exploded. Houses had broken into rubble. Cars were tossed upside down in trees. Poles had snapped as if they were splinters. How could anyone have survived this terrible tragedy? Families crept from basements and closets, school children huddled in hallways and bathrooms, and a baseball dugout sheltered some. Amid all that destruction, there was still faith in God and his mercy.

Out of wilderness experience our wonderful Lord gives us something to use to help others.

AMY CARMICHAEL, *EDGES OF HIS WAYS*

Here Am I, Send Me

Thank God for firefighters, for paramedics, for Red Cross teams, for police, for the National Guard, for search and rescue teams—for all who risk their lives for us, who step forward when we're hurting, who are there when we need them most.

In the arena of adversity, the Scriptures teach us three essential truths about God—truths we must believe if we are to trust him in adversity. They are:
—God is completely sovereign.
—God is infinite in wisdom.
—God is perfect in love.

JERRY BRIDGES, *TRUSTING GOD—EVEN WHEN LIFE HURTS*

One Christmas Morning

The apartments burned on Christmas Eve. No home, no tree, no gifts for those families and children. But the next morning, the city poured out love, toys, and gifts from countless hands to bring Christmas joy for bereft children.

Lord, Give me hope,
Give me patience to cope
And a reason to keep on trying.
Take my trembling hand
Give me power to stand
And a faith that is strong and undying.

BARBARA ROBERTS PINE, *"LORD, GIVE ME HOPE"*

Dear Lord, each night the news is full of trouble. So much pain and sorrow. It makes me ache to see it all. Some nights, it seems that's all there is; this world seems sometimes so weary and heavy laden. Then I turn to you and know that you are nearest on the darkest days. And there is comfort in knowing you and that you have not forsaken us or the people whose world is presently dark. Amen.

WATER'S RISING

Sarah watched in disbelief as the tiny, quiet creek behind her home swelled and spread. She'd never thought much about it before, never even thought of it as any sort of danger. Why should she? On a normal day she could easily step across it, maybe hop from one stone to another if it was wider after a heavy rain. But this time the tiny creek had swelled into an amazing turmoil of water, a rising flood that tightened her stomach every time she checked on it.

> *If the Lord had not been my help, my soul would soon have lived in the land of silence.*
>
> PSALM 94:17 NRSV

With a series of days of heavy rain and then the spring thaw on top of that, rivers and creeks were rising fast all across the state. She'd heard the news stories but hadn't thought all that much about it. She felt sorry for the people she saw gathering their belongings on trucks or piled atop family cars. She felt their grief as they left their homes, not knowing what sort of damage the swelling rivers would leave behind. She'd thought how hard it must be for them. Yet it hadn't truly touched her.

But now, with her own creek rising, she understood what those people were going through. She thought of floods she'd heard of—the huge floods when the Mississippi River washed away everything in its path, leaving only rooftops showing, cars floating like corks on a pond, and livestock stranded on hills. It seemed incredible that such devastation could happen here.

As she anxiously watched, the creek spread, creeping up across the park, covering the ball field, flowing over the length of the parking lot, and lapping at the base of her own yard. Frantically, she planned what to move to higher spots inside her home. Mentally, she inventoried belongings—what to save and what to leave behind if she were forced to evacuate.

She joined neighbors standing in their yards to check the water level and to offer guesses about how much farther their little creek could spread. Looking at her friends, she wondered if they'd all be in some shelter by nightfall. When a couple of young men paddled through the parking lot in a canoe, no one laughed or even smiled.

Inside her home, Sarah planned and prayed, watched and waited, thinking of all those people who'd already been flooded from their homes. And, at last, when the creek stopped rising and the water lapped gently just short of her door, she breathed a sigh of thankful relief. She and her household were untouched … this time.

God is our refuge and strength, an ever-present help in trouble.

PSALM 46:1 NIV

But she'd never take her blessings for granted again, never feel uninvolved when others suffered, never forget the reality that trouble could reach as easily into her own life as into anyone else's. She would always pray for the plight of others.

Disasters strike. Illnesses come. No time to prepare. Help us, Lord, stay close to you. Deepen our trust and faith in you. Amen.

Once God has touched us in the midst of our struggles and has created in us the burning desire to be forever united with him, we will find the courage and the confidence to prepare his way and to invite all who share our life to wait with us during this short time for the day of complete joy. With this new courage and new confidence we can strengthen each other with…hopeful words…

HENRI J. M. NOUWEN, *REACHING OUT*

Save me, O God,
for the floodwaters are up to my neck.
Deeper and deeper I sink into the mire;
I can't find a foothold to stand on.
I am in deep water,
and the floods overwhelm me.

I am exhausted from crying for help;
my throat is parched and dry.
My eyes are swollen with weeping,
waiting for my God to help me...
Answer my prayers, O Lord,
for your unfailing love is wonderful.

PSALM 69:1-3, 16 NLT

NOTHING CAN SEPARATE US

When disaster shatters our lives, God is our rock,
and nothing can separate us from him. Indeed,
nothing can separate us from his love.

Grant us wisdom,
Grant us courage,
For the facing of this hour,
For the facing of this hour.

HARRY EMERSON FOSDICK, "GOD OF GRACE AND GOD OF GLORY"

It Could Have Been Worse

Count your blessings, what you have, not what you've lost. It could have been worse. It could have been much worse.

All around, the storms may churn,
the seas may rage, the fires burn.
But deep within, you will not fear,
you will have peace when centered there.
For even amidst the tempest wild,
God will be there to guide you, Child.

Barbara Roberts Pine, "All Around, the Storms May Churn"

Oh Lord, when I see terrible, fearful events—mud slides destroying whole villages, droughts that turn crops to dust, storms devastating all in their path—then I turn to you. And you are always here, listening, caring, and waiting for all of us to reach out to you. Amen.

There is no darkness so great that Jesus cannot dispel it.

CORRIE TEN BOOM, A PRISONER AND YET...

Those who love me, I will deliver; I will protect those who know my name. When they call to me, I will answer them; I will be with them in trouble, I will rescue them and honor them.

PSALM 91:14-15 NRSV

CERTAIN COMFORT

Circumstances can cause our world to crumble around us. Yet we need not fall apart inside. If we place our trust in God's goodness, he will come to our aid and bring us comfort to restore our hope in the future. His love and compassion will lift our spirits so we can rejoice no matter what disaster or tragedy may befall us. For as long as God is beside us, nothing can defeat us or take what is truly important from us.

Thank you, Lord, for reaching out and drawing me under your wings. Even though I am just one of billions of people who need you, your love is so great that you know *my* troubles, are concerned for *my* welfare, and are working to renew *my* dreams. I am so blessed to have you to turn to when I am faced with a calamity, and I am so very grateful that I have you to lean on. I praise you with all my heart. Amen.

Let the words of my mouth and the meditation of my heart be acceptable to you, O Lord, my rock and my redeemer.

PSALM 19:14 NRSV

CHAPTER 2

THE DISCOURAGED SPIRIT

DISCOURAGEMENT COMES in many forms; no matter what the source, it exhausts the spirit and drains the soul. Without help, we feel as though we are drowning in a smothering well of darkness. Without hope, we want to give up. We want to give in. We want to wave the white flag of defeat.

When the obstacles that arise in our path seem insurmountable, and the challenges we face appear beyond our capability, that is when we most need to turn our lives over to a power greater than ourselves. Indeed, there is tremendous healing power in that moment of surrender, when our discouraged spirit feels it has reached its limit, for this is the moment when we are able to let go and let God take over.

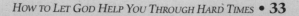

God's Mysterious Ways

For Debra, weight was a demon she was forced to wrestle with every day. Since childhood, Debra had been seriously overweight. Her mother often called her "cute and chubby," but she could see that she wasn't cute. She was fat and unattractive, and she hated herself for it.

When she entered adulthood, the struggle to control her burgeoning weight resulted in countless attempts to lose that weight. Occasionally, she could get her 5'3" body down to a reasonable weight of 160 to 170 pounds, only to balloon again back up to 250 pounds in a matter of months. Nothing seemed to work. It was taking every ounce of physical and emotional strength she had to keep trying, and her body was paying a dear price for her extreme shifts from starvation dieting to bingeing.

Eventually, Debra resigned herself to being obese. She knew people stared at her, talked about her behind her back, and belittled her. She was ashamed and full of self-loathing. She often prayed to God to help her, but she just kept gaining weight and wondered if her pleas had fallen on deaf ears. She truly felt there was no reason to live, and she began to seriously consider taking her life.

And so, it was seem-
ingly a fluke that she
came across a maga-
zine article that would

> *"He gives power to the faint and strengthens the powerless."*
> Isaiah 40:29 NRSV

ultimately lead her onto the road to healing and give new hope to her discouraged spirit. She came home from the market to find that the bag-boy had inadvertently put someone else's health magazine in with her groceries. She checked her receipt, saw she had not paid for it, and was about to take it back to the store when an article title on the cover caught her eye. It was about obesity.

Debra forgot about putting the food away and sat down to read the article. By the time she had finished, she had read it three times word for word. Meanwhile, tears were flowing freely down her cheeks and onto the pages of the magazine. It was as if something inside of her had burst open and was finally free.

Debra got up, went straight to her computer, and e-mailed the magazine editors, thanking them for printing this honest and life-affirming article. She poured out her heart and soul to these strangers. She wrote about how she, too, had battled with weight all her life. Like the author, she had been sexually abused by

> *Rejoice in hope, be patient in suffering, persevere in prayer.*
> ROMANS 12:12 NRSV

a close relative as a young girl and had struggled with a low self-image and the guilt and shame victims often experience from abuse. And, like the author, she had avoided intimacy with men, sure that they would find her body as repulsive as she did.

Unlike the author, however, Debra had never made the connection between her weight and the sexual abuse. Now, because of this one article, she finally began to understand why she had turned against her own body. It was a safety mechanism for her, a way not to attract unwanted sexual attention, and it had worked for her, but it was also destroying her.

Suddenly, Debra felt a renewed sense of encouragement and compassion for herself. She realized that God worked in mysterious ways and that he had placed this magazine in her hands. Indeed, God had heard her cry for help and responded. She felt an overwhelming sense of love as she sat there, holding the magazine in her trembling hands.

That night, Debra received a personal e-mail from the magazine's author. The two women became e-mail pen pals, and they pledged to support and assist each other through the long process of healing, especially with regard to the sexual abuse.

For Debra, a serendipitous event turned into a new friendship and a new chance at the life she had always wanted. She began her journey of emotional and physical healing all because of a stranger's story in a magazine she had never intended to buy but was obviously intended for her.

God, grant me the inner fortitude to meet my fears head on and the steadfast faith to refuse to be discouraged, even in the face of rejection. But most of all, God, grant me a heart that refuses to close itself off to love and gratitude, no matter how hopeless things may seem. Amen.

When you and I hurt deeply, what we really need is not an explanation from God but a revelation of God. We need to see how great God is; we need to recover our lost perspective on life. Things get out of proportion when we are suffering, and it takes a vision of something bigger than ourselves to get life's dimensions adjusted again.

WARREN W. WIERSBE, *WHY US?*
WHEN BAD THINGS HAPPEN TO GOD'S PEOPLE

HEALING WATERS

In my hour of need, I turn my eyes inward to a place where God's strength flows like a river of healing waters. I immerse myself in the current, and I am renewed.

When sometimes all has been dark, exceedingly dark…judging from natural appearances; yea, when I should have been overwhelmed indeed in grief and despair had I looked at things after the outward appearances…I have sought to encourage myself by laying hold in faith on God's almighty power, His unchangeable love, and His infinite wisdom.

BASIL MILLER QUOTING GEORGE MULLER,
MAN OF FAITH AND MIRACLES

GUIDING LIGHT

In the midst of the darkness that threatens to overwhelm us lies a pinpoint of light, a persistent flicker that guides us through the pain and fear, through the hopelessness and despair, to a place of peace and healing on the other side. This is God's Spirit, leading us back home like the lighthouse beacon that directs the ships through the fog to the safety of the harbor.

My Creator, blessed is your presence. For you and you alone give me power to walk through dark valleys into the light again. You and you alone give me hope when there seems no end to my suffering. You and you alone give me peace when the noise of my life overwhelms me. I ask that you give this same power, hope, and peace to all who know discouragement, that they, too, may be emboldened and renewed by your everlasting love. Amen.

AMAZING GRACE

God's grace is our comfort in times of trouble and our beacon of hope amid the blackness of despair. By opening ourselves to God's ever-present grace, we know we are loved and cared for, and our hearts sing out in joyful gratitude.

IN DUE SEASON

Stop moaning and asking, "Why, God, why?"
There is always a meaningful reason.
Stop whining and pleading, "When, God, when?"
For good things will arrive in due season.

We are promised that God's never early,
But neither is God ever late.
All the blessings we wish will come to us
When we learn to have faith while we wait.

When I am lost and discouraged,
And there seems to be no hope in sight,
I turn my cares over to the God of my heart,
And his love lets my spirit take flight.

Be encouraged, child of God. He loves you even in the midst of your pain. He loves you even when you don't love Him. He loves you when you feel utterly alone. He loves you with an everlasting love. Your suffering can take many things away from you—your health, your happiness, your prosperity, your popularity, your friends, your career, even your family. But there's one thing suffering can't take away; it can't take away the love of God.

RAY PRITCHARD, *THE ROAD BEST TRAVELED*

THE BEST MEDICINE

The best medicine for a discouraged spirit is a dose of love. Add a touch of support from friends and family, mix with a pinch of awareness of God's presence, and spread over your entire heart and soul. Wait ten seconds, then smile. Nothing can withstand such a powerful healing balm.

Creator, I know that my life has a purpose, but right now I seem to have lost my way. My head tells me that my existence has meaning, but right now my heart cannot discern what it is. I'm sure that I am loved, but right now my spirit is too tired to acknowledge it. I ask for direction to find my path again, discernment to understand my purpose, and a grateful heart to see all the blessings that already exist in my life, right now. Amen.

THERE IS A PLAN

Our discouraged spirit will once again know joy when we realize that there is a deeper reality to our lives, a level of truth only the heart can understand. That truth is this: There is a wonderful master plan at work in our lives, and that the One who guides our path loves us more than we can ever imagine. This, and this alone, is enough to make our spirits soar.

A DREAM THAT WOULD NOT DIE

There is nothing more tragic than watching a lifelong dream fade away. Since childhood, Sylvia had a passion for painting. It was her way of connecting to something greater and grander than herself. When she painted, she felt God's presence being expressed through her. She painted into early adulthood, even studying art in college, always believing that this was her purpose, but then she was forced to make a living. By her mid-twenties, her passion for painting had taken a backseat to a

> *Consider him who endured such opposition from sinful men, so that you will not grow weary and lose heart.*
>
> HEBREWS 12:3 NIV

full-time job, and eventually to a husband and two children.

Sylvia loved her family more than anything and knew they were her top priority, but something was still missing. There was a hole deep inside her she knew could be filled only by doing what she most loved to do.

Once married, Sylvia was able to work part-time since her husband, Jim, earned a good income. She was thrilled, thinking she would have more time to paint.

> *The Lord will guide you continually, and satisfy your needs in parched places, and make your bones strong; you shall be like a watered garden, like a spring of water, whose waters never fail.*
>
> ISAIAH 58:11 NRSV

Instead, her extra hours were filled up with taking the girls to after-school events, running errands, cleaning, and doing everything else but painting. Often she would pass by the well-worn easel and half-empty paint supplies, and her heart would ache for that feeling of freeing herself on the canvas. But then the phone would ring or the girls would call out, and she would simply close the door and attend to the latest crisis or concern.

As time went on, Sylvia had nearly forgotten her painting, but her heart continued to feel empty. She suffered bouts of anxiety and depression, and soon her mood swings were affecting everyone around her. When Jim sat down to talk to her about it, she insisted nothing was wrong, but that very night she lay in bed weeping softly and wondering why, with all the blessings she had, she was so unhappy and so unfulfilled. Before she finally fell asleep in exhaustion, she whispered a prayer to God, a prayer for clarity and understanding as to why she felt so discouraged. She closed the prayer by asking for guidance. Then she fell asleep.

The next morning began as usual, and Sylvia rushed to get the girls off to school. When she returned later that morning, there was a note from Jim on the refrigerator. All it said was "Guest Room." Sylvia scratched her head in confusion, then went upstairs and opened the door to the guest room. She gasped as she entered, for there sat a brand-new easel and an array of new paint supplies, all gaily bundled in big red bows. On the easel her husband had written: "Follow your dream, for that is where true happiness lies." As Sylvia moved closer and touched the easel, her eyes brimmed with tears. Just then Jim came into the room and held her close.

"Call to me and I will answer you."

JEREMIAH 33:3 NRSV

"God's not the only one who heard your prayer," he whispered. From that day on, Sylvia began painting every day. The change in her life and in her heart was as lovely to behold as one of her pictures.

BELOW THE SURFACE

It's easy to become tired and discouraged when we can see little or no progress being made toward our goals and dreams. Often, it looks as if nothing is happening, and we become frustrated and want to give up. But we must remember that although the surface of a pond often appears still and quiet, there is ever-abundant activity of life going on just below.

God, make me an open vessel through which the waters of your Spirit flows freely. Let your love move through me and out into my world, touching everyone I come in contact with. Express your joy through the special talents you have given me, that others may come to know your presence in their own lives by witnessing your presence in mine. Amen.

BREAKING THE CHAINS OF DISCOURAGEMENT

When someone we love is trapped in a prison of defeat and discouragement, we can help them break free of the chains that bind them by doing these three things: supporting their deepest dreams, believing in their gifts and talents, and loving and accepting them for who they are at this very moment.

We all live by hope. Disappointment occurs when hopes are not fulfilled, and in particular when we hope for the wrong things. We become disappointed when events do not turn out as we want or expect. Then our picture of the future is shattered. We wrestle with our own view of what is best compared to God's view of our best.... When we live under the lordship of Christ, our hopes are surrendered to Him.

JERRY WHITE, *CHOOSING PLAN A IN A PLAN B WORLD*

RELAX, GOD IS IN CHARGE

We become discouraged when we try to live according to our own time clocks. We want what we want, and we want it this very minute. Then, when we don't get it, we sink in the quicksand of hopelessness and defeat. Only when we realize that God is at work in our lives will we begin to relax and let things happen in due season. Fruit will not ripen any faster because we demand it but will ripen in all its sweet splendor when it is ready in spite of our demands.

Loving Creator, I ask that you bless my loved ones, for without them I would surely not have gotten through this. I see your light as a gentle glow in their eyes, and I know that they are your angels sent to guide my way. For this, I am blessed. Amen.

PIECES OF A DREAM

How often we mourn a shattered dream, a goal not met, a vision unfulfilled. Yet amid the pieces of one shattered dream often lie the makings of an even grander design for our life. What sometimes appears as a disappointing ending is, in truth, the beginning of a whole new and exciting road ahead.

Anyone can sing songs and be happy when all is well. But what happens when the dark day comes, when the valley stretches endlessly ahead, when illness racks, and when the bed is itself an affliction? That is when we glorify God, singing songs in the night, trusting in the goodness of the Lord.

W. A. CRISWELL, *ABIDING HOPE*

THE POWER OF CREATIVITY

The creative power within is your power to overcome any obstacle and break through any binding walls that keep you from your dreams. This power was given to you by the greatest of all creators, the One who created you, God. Just look around at the amazing beauty and diversity of the world you live in, and you will never again doubt that God supports your creative endeavors.

THE WINDOW OF OPPORTUNITY

When the door of one dream slams shut, and we feel trapped by the pain of resignation and disappointment, we must open our hearts and our eyes to see the windows just waiting to fling wide open. We will be led into a whole new realm of possibility if only we will believe. God does not take something away without giving something back in its place, and often what we are given back is even more wonderful than that which we lost.

ONE DAY AT A TIME

Jared walked into the smoky room and took a seat in the back. It was his fifth Alcoholics Anonymous meeting, and he still hadn't found the courage to sit up front or raise his hand to share. He had wanted to avoid going into rehab, which would have meant having to tell his boss and his close friends about his "problem with booze." So he decided to go alone. The funny thing was Jared knew his drinking was a secret to no one.

You who have made me see many troubles and calamities will revive me again; from the depths of the earth you will bring me up again. You will increase my honor, and comfort me once again.

PSALM 71:20-21 NRSV

This was his fourth attempt to get sober. He listened while people said you had to get a sponsor right away, work the steps, and talk to other alcoholics. They also stressed the most important key was finding a relationship with a power greater than yourself. Jared let it all go in one ear and out the other. The idea of having to bear his soul to a sponsor turned his stomach, and as for this God stuff, he wasn't buying it.

Tom, the leader of this particular meeting, had other plans. He looked point blank at Jared and asked him to share his story. Jared looked up, startled, and was about to give a weak excuse, but Tom kept prompting him to share. Jared thought of running out the door and not looking back when an overwhelming urge caused him to just start speaking. Suddenly, the words were flowing out

Be strong and courageous; do not be frightened or dismayed, for the Lord your God is with you wherever you go.

Joshua 1:9 NRSV

of him like lava, hot with anger and the pain of the past and his own father's alcoholism and abusive behavior. What was supposed to be a simple three-minute sharing turned into ten minutes of release as Jared spoke of things he had never told any other human being before. When he was silent, the room broke into hearty and supportive applause, and Jared knew he had made some kind of a breakthrough.

Jared listened to the stories of others, paying close attention to one gruff old biker, who spoke with reverence about his surrender to God and how it had saved his life. After the meeting, Jared felt drawn to the biker named Ray and meekly introduced himself. Ray didn't just shake Jared's hand; he embraced him. Jared felt more and more comfortable as they talked and asked Ray to sponsor him. Ray was honored and told Jared he would expect him to work hard at his sobriety, to attend meetings every week, to read the Big Book, to pray, and to turn his problem over to his Higher Power each morning.

Jared said he had never been able to rely on anything other than himself to get him sober. Ray laughed a hearty belly laugh and said, "That's why you failed. Your higher power can do for you what you cannot do for yourself. Just ask anyone who has ever overcome an addiction." Tom then stopped by, patted Jared on the back, and handed Jared a plastic token. On it were the words "One Day at a Time." Deep inside, Jared knew that this time it was going to work.

I WILL!

I WILL be strong in the face of weakness.
I WILL be brave in the face of fear.
I WILL persist in the face of failure.
I WILL stand again no matter how many times
   I fall.
I WILL follow my path no matter how often I lose
   my way.
I WILL live my dream no matter what obstacles
   stand before me.
I WILL be mighty.
I WILL be bold.
I WILL be what God intended me to be.
I WILL!

Lord, I am weary and cannot find my way. The nights seem endless and thick with a fog that engulfs my spirit, but I have faith in you, my Lord and my light. Faith that you will help me take another step when I feel I can no longer walk on my own. Faith that you will be the beacon of hope that guides my way through the darkness. Faith that this, too, shall pass and that I will know joy again. Amen.

REST IN ME

When the nights seem long, and the days feel like a struggle, and the spirit is weary, we find a resting place in God's enduring love, and we know that his plan for us is good. This is the true meaning of letting go and letting God's higher will be done in our lives.

Our hope is built on our Lord's faithfulness.

So we do not lose heart. Even though our outer nature is wasting away, our inner nature is being renewed day by day.

2 CORINTHIANS 4:16 NRSV

He's there with you now. Trust Him. And then expectantly anticipate that at the right time and in the way that's most creative to you and all concerned, He will intervene and infuse you with exactly what you need. What an exciting way to live!

Lloyd John Ogilvie, God's Best for My Life

ONLY A PRAYER AWAY

When we place ourselves into the care of a loving God, things that we once thought impossible now brim with possibility. That which had eluded us seems right within our grasp, and we rest in the knowledge that all the guidance and support we need is never more than a prayer away.

I shall know why, when time is over,
And I have ceased to wonder why;
Christ will explain each separate anguish
In the fair schoolroom of the sky.

He will tell me what Peter promised,
And I, for wonder at his woe,
I shall forget the drop of anguish
That scalds me now, that scalds me now.

EMILY DICKINSON, "THE MYSTERY OF BEAUTY"

SHARING THE BURDEN

So much of the crippling weight we carry upon our shoulders can be alleviated by simply understanding that we don't have to carry the burden alone. God is always there, walking beside us, and ready to take the entire load from us should we only ask Him to.

> *O Lord, you alone are my hope.*
>
> PSALM 71:5 NLT

God was there each step of the way. When we encountered the biggest obstacles and experienced the greatest discouragement, I felt his presence most.

DAPHNE GRAY, YES, YOU CAN, HEATHER!

Happiness is fleeting; it tends to depend on circumstances. Joy can be permanent. It is part of your character. A habit of grumbling and complaining, a tendency to be negative, tells something about the level of your spiritual life. Measure the Spirit's work in your life by your deep abiding joy regardless of life's circumstances.

WESLEY L. DUEWEL, *MEASURE YOUR LIFE*

Do not let your hearts be troubled. Believe in God, believe also in me.... Peace I leave with you; my peace I give to you. I do not give to you as the world gives. Do not let your hearts be troubled, and do not let them be afraid.

·JOHN 14:1, 27 NRSV

CHAPTER 3

WHEN LIFE IS OUT OF CONTROL

IT SEEMS AS IF the convenience culture has ushered us into a way of life that has an unprecedented level of day-to-day stress. Our time-saving devices and freedoms have inundated us with choices and busy-ness that never seem to end. How do we respond to the people and situations we encounter while living in a pressure-packed, fast-paced culture?

The illustrations and thoughts contained in this chapter will offer practical guidance and spiritual encouragement as you seek to navigate the twists and turns along the river of life. And you will find, as others have, that with God as your guide, you will find safe passage even when the waters seem to rage out of control.

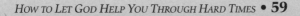

THE PLIGHT OF A "YES" PERSON

"Just say no!" Felicia chided her mother over the telephone.

"But Felicia, they really need someone to baby-sit and help them out of a last-minute predicament."

"Mom! How long will you keep pretending that you don't have a life of your own to attend to? I'm not talking about your own whims. I'm talking about the work around your house that you've been stressing out about—the cleaning, organizing, and painting? And you have relationships you need to tend to. You're already raising two grandkids, but everyone seems to think you're a free baby-sitting service!"

[Jesus said,] "Come to me, all you that are weary and are carrying heavy burdens, and I will give you rest."
MATTHEW 11:28 NRSV

"I know, but it's just for a few hours today, and—"

"And it's every day, just a few hours—the few hours you would be using to get caught up on things around here if you could. Isn't that right, Mom?"

"Well, yes. But they need me, and they're such nice people."

"Oh, Mom! You don't think you are allowed to say no, do you?" Felicia sighed in frustration.

God, so often we feel as though we're letting people down, as though we're failing if we don't answer all their requests and meet all their needs. Yet we know that things get out of balance in our own lives when we try to please everyone. We need you, today, to show us the path to more healthy ways of living and relating.

Who knows? If all of us slowed down a bit, if we cancelled a few meetings from the church calendar, if we took time to wait before God in prayer, we might see God work in wonderful ways. We might see some fractured marriages mended again, some discordant ministries brought back into God's harmony, some exhausted believers given new strength and zeal for God. We might even see revival!

WARREN WIERSBE, GOD ISN'T IN A HURRY

Lord, the clamor of my life is unbearable. People pressing in on all sides. Decisions crying out to be made. Problems needing to be solved. I don't want to get out of bed in the morning. I want to hide, to escape. Please help me!

HOW TO SPELL RELIEF

From the word stress, drop two s's and untangle the "rest."

We can let go of our worried grip on life. If we hang on to yesterday's troubles, tomorrow's fears, and today's anxieties, we will overload and blow the circuits.

LLOYD JOHN OGILVIE, GOD'S BEST FOR MY LIFE

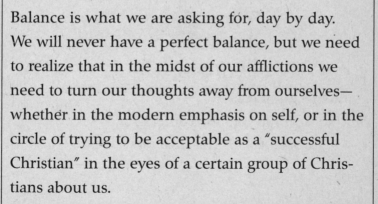

REALITY CHECK

While you're likely a super human being, that's not the same as being superhuman! Be who God made you to be.

God, when life feels like a ride that won't let us off, remind us that you are waiting for us to reach up to you. And when we finally do, thank you for being there to lift us to peace and safety.

Balance is what we are asking for, day by day. We will never have a perfect balance, but we need to realize that in the midst of our afflictions we need to turn our thoughts away from ourselves— whether in the modern emphasis on self, or in the circle of trying to be acceptable as a "successful Christian" in the eyes of a certain group of Christians about us.

EDITH SCHAEFFER, *AFFLICTION*

TIME FOR A VACATION?

"You with the bleary eyes, freeze! This is the sanity police. Listen carefully and no one'll get hurt: Put down that load, and step away from your problems. You're under arrest for illegally shouldering the world's weight. Let me take a look. Hey, I know you: a repeat offender, huh? You're gonna do some hard vacation time. Beach conditions in Hawaii are overcrowded, but you should've thought of that before you let it come to this. Hey, Charlie, take this one down to the airlines and book her!"

If God cares so much about you,
    there's good reason
        to begin to care for yourself.

TIM STAFFORD, *DO YOU SOMETIMES FEEL LIKE A NOBODY?*

God, in his mercy, allows us to confront our fears. In his kindness, he is trying to teach us to trust him, but that can be painful, and it's not at all obvious when it happens. That's because we're too caught up in what's going on to notice God is trying to teach us something.

LAURA LEE OLDHAM

A LITTLE GAS IN THE TANK

Imagine you're a driver whose car is running on just fumes. You have five bucks—not enough to fill the tank, but enough to keep you from becoming stranded. You're tempted, however, to save time and money, hoping against hope you'll make it home. In your life right now, a fill-the-tank kind of vacation may not be possible. But even an hour's enjoyment of a relaxing activity can prevent a regrettable setback. Stop and put a little gas into your tank today!

Long-legged and downy
It thunked to our porch
Complaining.
Silly Baby Crow.

Oh no!
It needs sustaining, maintaining, and all.

"Like my world,"
I recall
Flapping against fears
Fearing not to finish well.

In truth,
Small Crow flew to freedom
After so mighty a fall
And so might we all.

BARBARA ROBERTS PINE, "SILLY CROW"

[Jesus] entered a certain village, where a woman named Martha welcomed him into her home. She had a sister named Mary, who sat at the Lord's feet and listened to what he was saying. But Martha was distracted by her many tasks; so she came to him and asked, "Lord, do you not care that my sister has left me to do all the work by myself? Tell her then to help me." But the Lord answered her, "Martha, Martha, you are worried and distracted by many things; there is need of only one thing. Mary has chosen the better part, which will not be taken away from her."

LUKE 10:38-42 NRSV

MY "MARTHA COMPLEX"

I looked around the room in dismay. It was December 27, and I had told my landlord I would be out of my apartment by December 30. (Because of my financial situation, I had to move to Canada temporarily.) With Christmas just over and all of my commitments related to the holidays finally met, I had only a couple of days now to pack, put everything in storage, winterize my car for the cold Calgary months ahead, find a home for my cat, and take care of many other last-minute details before heading north. Besides these and other tasks, I had decided to work at my two part-time jobs up to the last day.

Some of my dilemma lay in the fact that things had become complicated since the time I'd first laid out my plans. Family members, who had promised me their help (and their van) for moving, had left that very week (with the van) to tend to an out-of-state family emergency. The people who'd said they would care for my cat had backed out of the agreement on the day before Christmas.

Yet, even if there had been no setbacks, there was the bottom-line reality: This time I had bitten off more than I could chew, and I was choking on a mouthful of to-do's. In desperation, I called a long-time friend: "Would you please come help?" I begged.

> *Cast all your anxiety on him, because he cares for you.*
> 1 PETER 5:7 NRSV

"No problem," she said without hesitation.

For three evenings straight, Megan showed up. Late into the nights she stayed, making numerous trips with me back and forth (in the cold and damp December fog) to the storage area I had rented. Often as Megan and I worked, I would stop and stand in the middle of a room, running my fingers through my messy hair, trying to focus and decide which job to tackle next. Megan just kept working, and when she noticed a blank expression on my face, she would gently help me think through what needed to be done.

Despite my friend's kindness, I was in a foul mood the whole time, sad and angry that I couldn't find a suitable place for my cat. At one point, I walked over to her and began to cry. "I'm so sorry about my bad mood, Megan," I shook my head. "Could you just take a minute and pray for me?" Putting her hand on my shoulder, Megan prayed for me. I sensed my friend's genuine concern and care, as though an extension of God's own. It was a moment of calm in the storm.

I wish I could say prayer changed everything, that I was suddenly whistling tunes from *Mary Poppins* and feeling chipper. The truth is, the next day, just 15 hours before departing for Canada, I drove to the vet with my cat. All my avenues had been exhausted. Her nervous temperament and delicate stomach caused her to vomit on a regular basis: something I just couldn't overlook telling potential caretakers, and something potential caretakers were unwilling to overlook. I could not leave her at a shelter; she never would have survived emotionally. As I choked out an explanation of my situation to the vet, he listened understandingly. Minutes later, I left, wiping away my tears.

I put in my last hours at my part-time housecleaning job and then returned to my apartment, where I found Megan already scrubbing out my oven. My eyes were red and swollen, and I had a booming headache. But there was still much to do: more trips to storage, more cleanup, and my car to pack.

Megan was there to the bitter end, and when we looked for a place to eat some dinner at 11:30 that night, she didn't say a word about having to get up early the next morning for work.

"I tried to do too much in too little time again," I admitted. "Someday, maybe I'll get real about what's possible in 24 hours, huh? I'm sorry I put you through this."

"Hey, don't worry about me. And stuff like this happens once in a while," Megan said. "But you don't want to be living your life this way, you know?"

"Yeah, I know."

Be still, and know that I am God!
PSALM 46:10 NRSV

It was silent a few moments before I spoke again. "Most of all I need to have time to be quiet and still. To listen to God. I haven't done that much lately, and I really miss it."

"I guess it's human nature," Megan noted, "to listen to the thing that's shouting the loudest instead of being intentional about hearing the thing that is most important."

The next morning, during the first leg of my 15-hour drive northeast, I thought a lot about the previous several days and about my conversation with Megan. *I've got a serious "Martha Complex,"* I assessed, thinking of the Bible's account of the sisters with differing priorities. *And Megan's right, I don't want to be living this way.*

It was time to break my pattern. With the following day being New Year's Eve, I had an idea for a personal resolution worth following through on: This year, I will seek to become a bit more like Mary and give the Martha in me a much-needed rest.

Jesus Christ is the only One Who is perfectly whole and healthy and balanced and normal. And the more you fix your eyes on Him, the more whole and healthy and balanced and normal you will be.

ANNE ORTLUND, *FIX YOUR EYES ON JESUS*

Father, thank you for the people you've placed in my life who express their concern for me. It's hard sometimes to lay down my pride and accept their help. I know, though, that when I gratefully receive from them, they in turn, receive affirmation that I trust them and value their friendship.

We work, we pull, we struggle, and we plan until we're utterly exhausted, but we have forgotten to plug into the source of power. And that source of power is prayer—the "effectual fervent prayer" of a righteous person that avails much.

EVELYN CHRISTENSON (WITH VIOLA BLAKE), *WHAT HAPPENS WHEN WOMEN PRAY*

GOD IN DISGUISE?

When we cry out to God for help, are we prepared to receive what he offers when he comes to us in the disguise of our friends and neighbors?

Thank you for some release, some sleep. I will be an instrument of your love. Now I am in need of tremendous strengthening. I implore. Give me your strength for my body. Fill me anew with your joy and love. I need help in so many things. Yard is overrun. House needs painting....I am so tired. Completely depleted.

KAREN BURTON MAINS, *KAREN! KAREN!*

Lord, we don't like to let stress destroy our even keel, but sometimes it does. We need your wisdom to help us manage the load and your grace to keep us from being ill-tempered.

TAKE A DRINK

If life is a marathon, we are wise to know our limits, to run within them, and to accept those blessed cups of water from time to time, offered by encouragers and God.

How can we be afraid or worried when we belong to such a wonderful God!...He knows everything and cannot make a mistake. He is everywhere and will not leave us or forsake us. He can do anything and is able to deal with the wickedness of this world in His own way and time.

Oh, the wonder of it all!

WARREN WIERSBE, *MEET YOURSELF IN THE PSALMS*

So often I convince myself that I can't afford the time it takes to quiet my heart and listen to you, Lord. But the truth is, I can't afford the toll it takes on my life not to listen. Please help me stop today and receive the rest and renewal you provide as I spend time in your presence.

THE PROVISION

Cameron had lost his job due to company downsizing. Because he was always industrious and reliable, Cameron was taken off guard when the pink slip landed on his desk. "I'd never been fired in my life," he said dejectedly. Moreover, since many companies were laying off employees in Cameron's area of expertise, it was not a good time to be looking for a job.

As the sole provider for his wife and two growing sons, Cameron didn't have long to be out of work before the family's savings would be depleted. The unemployment checks were not nearly enough to meet the monthly budget, but days and then weeks came and went until several months had passed, and Cameron could not secure even an interview in his specialized field of experience and training.

"The stress was tremendous, and it was having a negative effect on our family life," Cameron confessed. "I began to have an urgent sense that if I didn't change my perspective and attitude, we weren't going to make it through."

Cameron and his wife spent long hours talking about what they needed to do to hold things together. Finally, based on what they knew about God's promises and their situation, they decided they had to make a sincere effort to stop worrying about what would happen and, instead, start praying and taking God at his word.

Together Cameron and his wife made a list of their debts and bills and the amount they needed to meet each, and together they spent time each day asking God to guide Cameron's search for work and to provide for the family's needs. "When we put our energies into whatever God gave us to do and didn't sweat what the future would bring, an amazing calm came over our household," Cameron said. "Odd jobs kept opening up for me to do. And I always had just enough work to meet the financial obligations we had."

As an act of gratitude and trust in God's promise to provide for his family's needs, Cameron gave a certain percentage of his income to a nonprofit organization that reached out to needy people in the community. "I couldn't help but give. God was so faithful to us. During the entire time I was out of work, our car never broke down, my children's clothes and shoes did not wear out, we had no unexpected or emergency expenses, and there was always just enough money to pay the bills and put food on the table. God took care of us in every way."

[Jesus said to his followers,] "I tell you, do not worry about your life, what you will eat, or about your body, what you will wear. For life is more than food and the body more than clothing."
Luke 12:22-23 NRSV

Cameron's "odd jobs" evolved into a home business that specializes in estimating damages and doing cleanup for small businesses that experience floods, fires, and other similar disasters. As a team, Cameron and his wife take care of all aspects of the company, and they have enjoyed moderate success in their business.

"I'm not rich," Cameron smiles, "but it's a living, and we're still here."

As far as Cameron is concerned, that year of nip-and-tuck living was a seminar in learning to let go of the illusion of being in control of his own life and finding what it really means to trust God's provision. "When you have a family counting on you to feed them, to give them a house to live in, and to buy the clothes they need, it becomes a heavy load when you lose the means to do that. But that's the very thing that brought me face to face with the reality that I need God's help to be able to meet the responsibilities he has given me."

"It's not an experience I'd care to repeat," Cameron chuckled, "but it's not one I would trade for a million dollars. It may sound clichéd, but money cannot buy the personal growth nor the insights that I gained during that struggle. And the best part is that God has become so much more real to me. Seeing his intervention in my life made me know that God's love is not just theoretical or for everyone else. Now I believe beyond a shadow of a doubt that he cares about me, too."

Get a new vision of God's love for you. Although God loves the whole world, He loves you personally. He is your God. He wants to be your God in greater reality than ever before.

WESLEY L. DUEWEL, *MEASURE YOUR LIFE*

Lord, help me not to accuse you of being untrue when I don't get from you everything I want, for you have promised to meet all my needs. And when I learn to love you supremely and trust you wholly, my desires will find fulfillment in you.

We must live knowing that God is perfecting the good work that he has begun in us and that he will bring it to completion. We must take the pilgrimage of life as the adventure that it is—as we work and play, travel and travail, read good books and climb high mountains, have our babies and bury our dead. Never satisfied, we must be still and still moving into another intensity, a further union, a deeper communion.

Kelly James Clark

Our Provider

One of the Hebrew names for God is Jehovah Jireh (JY-rah). Besides having a nice ring to it, its meaning—"God, our provider"—is one worth remembering. In life, we may experience times of abundance and also times when we struggle to make ends meet. In any situation, God asks us to trust and honor him as Jehovah Jireh, the God who provides all that we truly need.

…From then on I followed the daily practice of prayer in earnest. There were no delays, no short-cuts. I knew that my mother was right. The practice of praying in the morning set the pace for the rest of the time of day.

DAVID C. COOK, *INVISIBLE HALOS*

TIME TO GO HOME?

Money rolled in and the living was fine:
God was in his place, and I safe in mine.
But something went wrong; now bills stand in
   piles.
I guessed I'd call God from "across the miles."
I expected he'd moved, but he was still there—
Said I could return and find rest in his care.
"But money!" I cried. "That's my problem now;
I've got to pay bills, and I don't quite know how."
On the heels of my lament came his quiet reply:
"Dear child, just come home; at the right time, I'll
   supply."

Don't fret or worry. Instead of worrying, pray. Let petitions and praises shape your worries into prayers, letting God know your concerns. Before you know it, a sense of God's wholeness, everything coming together for good, will come and settle you down. It's wonderful what happens when Christ displaces worry at the center of your life.

PHILIPPIANS 4:6-7 *THE MESSAGE*

DON'T FAIL TO PRAY

Some people say, "When all else fails, pray," but wise folks never wait that long.

Give your life with all its stress to Him and say, "Lord, please give me a new life. Replace the pressure I feel with the peace You offer. Help me follow Your principles of stress management."

RICHARD WARREN, *ANSWERS TO LIFE'S DIFFICULT QUESTIONS*

Dear Lord, my financial demands exceed the resources I have. The pressure I feel to do something, even if it's unwise, is building, and I fear I will cave in and make a decision I will regret. Help me trust you. Preserve my integrity and show me your way of dealing with this situation.

I Wonder

I look around and see people who seem to own every imaginable thing money can buy. And I wonder, if I were in their shoes, would I ever experience the joy of an unexpected gift from an understanding friend? Would I ever pray to God in desperation and learn from within my need how much he has to offer? Would I ever recognize the pain of another struggling soul and be compelled to offer my concern and help? I wonder.

Our only task is to keep in step with him. He chooses the direction and leads the way. As we walk step by step with him, we soon discover that we have lost the crushing burden of needing to take care of ourselves and get our own way, and we discover that the burden is indeed light. We come into the joyful, simple life of hearing and obeying.

RICHARD J. FOSTER, *FREEDOM OF SIMPLICITY*

THE BEGINNING OF FAITH

All too often it is not until we reach our rope's end that we find an opportunity for the beginning of faith.

Those who hope in the Lord will renew their strength. They will soar on wings like eagles; they will run and not grow weary, they will walk and not be faint.

ISAIAH 40:31 NIV

CHAPTER 4

HEALING A WOUNDED HEART

EMOTIONAL WOUNDS may leave no visible physical scars, but deep within, a heart can be suffering. A love gone bad, a relationship that is filled with conflict, shattered friendships, a grudge that will not be settled—they all bring just as much agony as do disasters and physical illnesses.

A special kind of healing is called for when dealing with the wounds of the heart. This must be a healing based on forgiveness, acceptance, and release. To be able to forgive someone who has caused us pain or to let go of a deep resentment requires a maturity and charity that few of us are able to find within ourselves. That is when we need to call upon God, for only God has the power to help us truly forgive and to heal our wounded hearts.

THE TIES THAT BIND

Grace was only 15 when she watched her father pack his things and walk out the door and out of her life with nothing but a quick kiss on the cheek. She was old enough to understand the basics of divorce: Two people who once had been in love no longer felt they were able to live together. Yet what Grace was unable to understand, or forgive, was the fact that her father had chosen to completely cut ties with her and her younger sister, Eileen.

> *Even if my father and mother abandon me, the Lord will hold me close.*
> PSALM 27:10 NLT

The two girls literally grew into their adulthood without the man they had once worshiped and adored. Throughout childhood, Grace had been "daddy's girl," and Eileen was "the apple of his eye," but, as the years went by, he became an invisible specter, a presence they could still feel, but never actually see. Their relationship with him went from occasional visits every six months, to letters, to quick and impersonal phone calls. He moved to another part of the country, and eventually, when Grace was in her late 20s, her father remarried. That was the last she heard from him.

When Grace turned 40, she felt a resurgence of her earlier anger, which she had often suppressed toward her father. What she had thought she had come to accept in her father's behavior, she now realized she did not accept at all. In fact, it made her furious. She could see his needing to make a complete split from her mother, but why did he feel the need to throw his children away in order to start a new life? Did he not love his daughters? Was the new woman he married planning to give him new daughters to call his own?

As time went by, Grace suffered debilitating migraine headaches. She went to several doctors seeking help when one nurse practitioner had the intuitive wisdom to read more into Grace's painful migraines than just a physical cause. She and Grace talked about things that might be "gripping her brain like a vise," as the nurse put it. That's when Grace finally realized that if she didn't come to some kind of resolution with her father, she would suffer more than just migraines. Moreover, she had to do it for Eileen as well, for she discovered that Eileen was struggling with alcohol dependency and depression. Grace was certain she knew why.

She had often laughed over her parents' choice for her name, but now Grace knew that "grace" was exactly what she needed to be to make this situation right for all involved. She prayed and asked her heavenly Father to guide and strengthen her; she journaled and finally felt God leading her to contact her father. It began with a simple e-mail, asking how he was doing. He must have been sitting by his computer, because the response came immediately. "Please call me. I would love to hear that lilt in your voice that always made my spirits soar." Grace could not believe it when she read

> *Be kind to one another, tenderhearted, forgiving one another, as God in Christ has forgiven you.*
> EPHESIANS 4:32 NRSV

those words. Had he, indeed, remembered her voice at all? She summoned all the courage she could receive from God, and one week later, she called her father.

When she heard his voice, she broke into a rage of tears, which she could not control. It was as if a dam had burst and there was nothing she could do to stop the angry words, the questions wrapped in fury and resentment. Why did you leave us? Why don't you love us? What did we do to make you go away? All of the questions she had wanted to ask that day long ago when she was 15 flowed out of her like liquid magma.

After a period of silence when Grace could tell her father was weeping, he whispered quietly, "I was afraid, and ashamed, and I didn't have the courage to face the two girls I loved so much. I thought you hated me, and I didn't know how to deal with that hate. I thought you wouldn't want anything to do with me, and I couldn't deal with that."

As their conversation continued, Grace began to understand that her father had disappeared because he did not have the emotional strength or fortitude to deal with the situation. It was a weak excuse, but it was honest. In a way, he had always been hoping his strong and beautiful daughters would make that first move—the one he was just too scared and too ashamed to make.

That conversation led to her father flying out to meet Grace and Eileen to make amends, and the day was filled with tears of anger, grief over years lost, release, forgive-

> *Let us therefore approach the throne of grace with boldness, so that we may receive mercy and find grace to help in time of need.*
> HEBREWS 4:16 NRSV

ness, and finally love. Grace learned that relationships really never end, they just change, and that sometimes the change can be an experience of tremendous growth for all involved. From that day onward, her migraines ended, but more importantly her father became a presence in her life again, and their loving relationship rekindled by forgiveness reminded her of the remarkable grace of her heavenly Father.

Dear God, the wound between this person and me seems too deep to heal, and the chasm of misunderstanding seems too wide to leap across. I pray for guidance that I may do my part to close the wound and narrow the gap between us with love, understanding, and forgiveness. Amen.

Unforgiveness is an acid which does more damage to the vessel in which it is stored than the victim on which it is poured. I had to face the fact that my emotional and spiritual, as well as physical, healing waited on my determination to forgive.

BARBARA TAYLOR, *FROM REJECTION TO ACCEPTANCE*

SECOND CHANCES

Everyone deserves a second chance, a chance to start anew with the slate wiped clear of past mistakes. If someone you love has hurt you, remember that God has forgiven you. Then forgive and move on to a new level of relationship.

In your own pain and tragedy, you are being invited to enter into a closer relationship with God. Whatever may or may not happen to your children, great good and enormous enrichment can come into your own life if only you will draw near to God.... You can pass through fire and come out as fine gold. You can become more truly alive, more aware. Your very pain brings with it the possibility of untold riches.

JOHN WHITE, *PARENTS IN PAIN*

God, I pray for the strength and the wisdom to know what to do in this situation. I pray for enough love to forgive this person for the pain they have caused me, and to forgive myself for the ill will I have harbored against this person. Help me be a truly forgiving person so that the weight of resentment may be lifted from my shoulders. Amen.

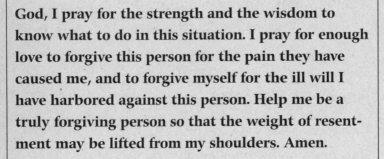

When we walk along a clear road feeling fine, and someone takes our arm to help us, as likely as not we shall impatiently shake him off; but when we are caught in a rough country in the dark, with a storm getting up and our strength spent, and someone takes our arm to help us, we shall thankfully lean on him. And God wants us to feel that our way through life is rough and perplexing, so that we may learn thankfully to lean on him.

J. I. PACKER, *KNOWING GOD*

THE GIFT OF FORGIVENESS

The greatest gift we can offer someone is our forgiveness, for it has the dual power to set the other person free and to set us free as well.

Whether my pain is self-inflicted through sin or stupidity or imposed by the hurts that others cause, his grace brings redemption.

JOHN F. WESTFALL, *ENOUGH IS ENOUGH*

There are times when our prayer concerns are simply too heavy. We are especially vulnerable with our children, because our hearts are so bound up in them. And yet we must pray with a sense of giving them to Him.... And even though the unbearable may happen,... we can pray honestly and deeply, releasing the burden into His care.

NANCIE CARMICHAEL, *DESPERATE FOR GOD*

MADE IN GOD'S IMAGE

Love opens our hearts to a clarity of vision that sees beyond another person's flaws, mistakes, and shortcomings. Love helps us see what God is doing in our lives. Love helps us see God more clearly in ourselves.

The love of God is evident
in every soul we meet.
For we are but the vehicles
through which God moves his feet.

THE GARDEN OF LOVE

Sow seeds of kindness by first planting your thoughts in the rich and fertile soil of love. Then, with the warmth of God's love and light, watch those thoughts bloom into a rich harvest of acts of caring and compassion.

Oh Lord, I do not know how to deal with this person. I am afraid and angry, and my heart aches with sadness. I turn to you, God, and ask for the peace that passes all understanding. I surrender the yoke of my burden to you, that your will be done, not mine. Let me rest in the healing waters of your ever-present Spirit, now and forever. Amen.

No matter what deep hurt you have experienced, He is able to redeem it. If you allow Jesus to walk with you.…He will take your valley of trouble and give you a *Door of Hope*.

JAN FRANK, *DOOR OF HOPE*

BLESSING IN DISGUISE

Meredith had never held a grudge against anyone, let alone her brother, Paul. They had always had a good relationship, talking often despite living a thousand miles apart. Then, when their mother passed away, only three years after their father had died, the two of them were called to settle the will. Apparently, their mother had left the entire wealthy estate to Paul, also appointing him to be executor to decide what Meredith should inherit. It was another slap in the face to Meredith, who had always known that her mother had preferred Paul to her. Meredith had been independent and had forged a life for herself as a writer, which did not include living within a ten-minute drive of her mother. It was something her mother never let Meredith forget.

To Meredith, however, it had been the only way she knew to make a life of her own, free from the oppressive glare of her mother's eyes. Now, she was about to be told once again that she meant nothing to her mother. She had expected it, but she never thought Paul would be so cruel as to completely cut her out of any of their parents' estate. Yet, that was exactly what he was doing, telling his sister that he was only following their mother's wishes.

Meredith thought about suing for her share. She even called Paul's sweet wife, Becky, thinking she

> *Let us then pursue what makes for peace and for mutual upbuilding.*
> ROMANS 14:19 NRSV

might be able to convince Paul to be a little more generous, but Becky proved to be ineffectual against Paul. And the sneaky phone call to his wife made Paul even more furious at Meredith. As time went on, Meredith could feel the hostility and resentment build up inside of her to a boiling point, and she knew if she did not do something, it would make her sick.

Never having been a religious person, Meredith suddenly felt compelled to call upon the help of something bigger and wiser than herself. She actually dropped to her knees and prayed to God.

After a long moment, Meredith found a peacefulness envelop her, which she had never felt before. She stayed on her knees for a long, long time and just let the answer flow into her consciousness like a river.

The answer, she realized, was not to sue or confront Paul, not to rage and rant and moan. The answer was to accept it, which made no sense intellectually, but in her heart she knew it was the right thing to do if she ever wanted peace in her life.

She called Paul that night and left a message on his machine, asking him to forgive her for her behavior and telling him with love and sincerity that she had totally accepted the outcome of the will. Within two days, Paul called Meredith, not only asking for her forgiveness, but also begging her to let him come stay with her awhile. After Paul arrived, they spent every day talking about their lives, their parents, and expectations and dreams. Paul confessed he had always resented Meredith for her courage to break away and pursue her dreams. Now he had the money and the freedom to do the same, but he still lacked the courage.

By the end of his visit, Paul had eagerly and lovingly signed over half the estate to his sister, but even more importantly, Meredith had given Paul an equal amount of courage to finally be his own man. For both Paul and Meredith, it was a blessing they knew they might never have received had Meredith not turned to the One who heals broken relationships.

Be completely humble and gentle; be patient, bearing with one another in love. Make every effort to keep the unity of the Spirit through the bond of peace.
EPHESIANS 4:2-3 NIV

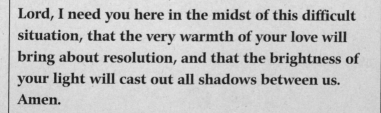

Lord, I need you here in the midst of this difficult situation, that the very warmth of your love will bring about resolution, and that the brightness of your light will cast out all shadows between us. Amen.

THE POWER OF KINDNESS

We will truly have the most loving, joy-filled relationships when we finally learn that always being kind is much more important than always being right.

When people disappoint or hurt me, remind me to look at you, Lord, instead of them.

LOIS WALFRID JOHNSON, *YOU'RE MY BEST FRIEND, LORD*

Love makes us greater
than we ever were before,
takes what we have to give
and gives back even more.

Love makes us stronger
than we ever thought we'd be,
takes the load we have to bear
and sets our spirits free.

Lord, I am hurting now, to the point of numbness. The only comfort I truly have at this moment is knowing that you are gently holding me in your arms. It makes me realize that you have always been faithful to get me through the storms. This gives me the confidence and comfort to carry on.

CHARLES STANLEY, *A TOUCH OF HIS GRACE*

THE WISEST COUNSELOR

When conflict and anger threaten to tear our family apart, the solution lies in turning to God as a wise counselor whose intuitive guidance and wisdom can bring us back to unity and wholeness again.

Certainly God brings healing, forgiveness, and renewal to all who confess their human failings to him with a repentant heart.

CHARLES COLSON, *AGAINST THE NIGHT*

As We Give, We Receive

As we let go of resentment, others let go of their resentment toward us. As we forgive, we are also forgiven. As we learn to accept and tolerate differences, others will accept and tolerate ours. By showing mercy, instead of meanness, we receive the blessing of mercy in return.

When our will is surrendered to God and all its action flows from the power plant of God's will, then disappointment becomes His appointment, and life is no longer a ceaseless struggle to get Him to do something that we think He ought to do.

ALAN REDPATH, *VICTORIOUS CHRISTIAN LIVING—STUDIES IN THE BOOK OF JOSHUA*

Thank you, God, for the people you have chosen to be my family and my friends. They are my guides, my teachers, my angels, and my cheerleaders. Though I may often be in conflict with them, and we fight and argue and say things we will regret, I am blessed to have these people walking beside

me along life's path, helping me to grow and become who you created me to be. Amen.

Jesus knows this feeling of being let down by
friends. In the worst hour of one night, he struggled until sweat trickled down his forehead like
drops of blood. And his best friends slept...

So God knows how much we need his absolute
promise that he does not sleep through our times
of pain. And he has given us his word. No matter
how alone we may feel, we are never alone. We
always have his company.

JANE GRAYSHON, *IN TIMES OF PAIN*

PSALM 121

I lift up my eyes to the hills–
    from where will my help come?
My help comes from the Lord,
    who made heaven and earth.

He will not let your foot be moved;
    he who keeps you will not slumber.

He who keeps Israel
   will neither slumber nor sleep.

The Lord is your keeper;
   the Lord is your shade at your right hand.
The sun shall not strike you by day,
   nor moon by night.

The Lord will keep you from all evil;
   he will keep your life.
The Lord will keep your going out and your
      coming in
   from this time on and forevermore.

If there is one thing that pain or sorrow will do for
a Christian, it is to enlarge his capacity for God. In
the desperation of our need we reach out for Him;
we throw ourselves upon His mercy and cling to
Him in our helplessness. In doing so, are we not
being prepared, all unwittingly, to enjoy more
completely the joys of heaven—in effect, to "take
heaven" now?

MARGARET CLARKSON, *GRACE GROWS BEST IN WINTER*

TO BEGIN AGAIN

Dana had considered her marriage to be strong and solid. Jack was a bit controlling and critical of her, but basically they got along well. The thought of divorce had never entered her mind, even during their most vocal fights. So when he came to her one day and told her he was leaving and that he was in love with another woman, she thought the ground had vanished from beneath her.

The day Jack packed up and walked out remained a blur in Dana's mind for months afterward, especially after she discovered

He heals the brokenhearted and binds up their wounds.
PSALM 147:3 NIV

Jack had been seeing a mutual good friend of theirs for over two years. She lost a husband, a friend, and her trust in people in one fell swoop.

After a long period of grieving and trying to understand why it had happened, Dana decided the only way she could find peace and move on was to confront Jack and ask him what had gone wrong between them. When she did, Jack treated her coldly, telling her he had never been happy and that they should never have married in the first place. Dana was so anguished that she failed to hear the still, small voice within her telling her Jack was right.

She then began to pray, desperately seeking answers. After a few days, Dana could feel a calming presence watching over her when she prayed, and she heard a clear voice telling her she was and always would be deeply loved.

> *He will yet fill your mouth with laughter, and your lips with shouts of joy.*
>
> JOB 8:21 NRSV

Dana slowly picked up the pieces of her life, starting with going back to the church she once loved but stopped attending because Jack didn't like it; taking classes she had always wanted to take, but never had time for; calling old friends she had drifted away from after she got married. She realized how much of herself she had left behind when she married Jack. She received a clarity that saw beyond the illusion of her "perfect marriage," which, under honest scrutiny, suddenly didn't look that good after all, and she knew Jack was right: They never should have married; they were far too different. What seemed a tragedy became an incredible learning and growing experience for Dana.

Although single life was scary, Dana knew she was never really alone. She had family, good friends, and the love of God on her side. She even let herself be open to one day falling in love again, only this time she would not lose herself in the bargain.

Lord,
If like a fragile flower
Torn petal by petal
My heart must continue to tear
Let there be fragrance.

RUTH HARMS CALKIN, "FRAGRANCE," KEEP ME FAITHFUL

THE RESILIENT HEART

When someone breaks our heart, we mourn, we grieve, and we feel the pain of rejection. We pray to God for healing and relief. And then we pick up the pieces and, with God's help and guidance, rebuild a heart that is even stronger, more resilient, and ready to love again.

If your heart has been shattered and broken
and your spirit is crippled with pain,
you can call on the God of all comfort
to heal you to wholeness again.

If the ground is hard, the rain rolls off. But if the ground is broken, then the rain can soak in and moisten the earth. We've been broken, too...so that God can let His healing power flow down through us.

DOUG WEAD, *A TIME TO LIVE*

Moving Past Resentment

Forgiveness is not easy. Often it requires us to become far more than we were before; more mature, more accepting, and more compassionate. But once we forgive and stretch ourselves, we can never go back to being that unforgiving and resentful person we were before. We have been opened up, expanded, and set free.

God, hear my prayer. Bless me with patience and a steadfast heart to help me get through such emotionally trying times. Heal the wounds of my heart and soul with the soothing balm of your comforting presence, that I may be able to love and to live again. Amen.

How else but through a broken heart
  May Lord Christ enter in?

Oscar Wilde, "The Ballad of Reading Gaol"

Jesus said, "Very truly, I tell you, you will weep and mourn…you will have pain, but your pain will turn into joy."

JOHN 16:20 NRSV

Dear Lord, thank you for healing my heart and bringing joy and meaning back into my life. Thank you for the people who truly care for me. Help me be a soothing and joyful presence in their lives as well. Amen.

CHAPTER 5

THE PROBLEM WITH PAIN

PAIN, IN ITS COUNTLESS FORMS, can test us to our limits; it can seem to over-whelm us at times and plunge us into discouragement and even despair. Is it possible for us to handle such debilitating pain? The kind that's always there, every morning, every night—pain that's relentless?

The answer is that it is possible. When it hurts too much to even pray, when pain overwhelms us, God is present—close and caring—even before we are able to ask. God can and will get us through. He provides friends to encourage us and pray for us, doctors and medicine to heal us, and the faith and strength we need to conquer whatever pain we face.

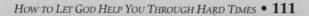

CAN'T BREATHE!

Waking in the lonely darkness of night, I gasped for air, fighting to breathe, feeling pain sear through my aching lungs. Fear clutched me. What if my lungs tightened so that I couldn't breathe at all? What if I couldn't even draw breath to call for help? What if nobody came to help me, and I died there alone in the night?

The fear wasn't new to me. Not being able to breathe brings a special terror many people don't understand. For most people, breathing isn't even something they think about. It's taken for granted, as normal as walking, talking, and eating. For me, breathing was a gift to be treasured and appreciated because there were terrible times when every breath came as a struggle.

The pain might strike me for almost no apparent reason. A puff of dust in my face. A whiff of dry laundry detergent. An especially cold day with air so frigid that it tightened my lungs. Even powdered drink mix might cause my lungs to tighten and my breathing to rasp.

The worst, though, were those horrible nights when I'd abruptly jolt awake, unable to catch my breath, feeling that ominous tension in my chest. Who knew why asthma struck while I slept, but it often did, and I was never entirely braced for it. I knew that fear and tension would only make it worse, but not being able to breathe always caught me off guard and terrified me.

I'd grown up with asthma, with emergency visits to the doctor, with shots, and with small purple pills tucked under my tongue. I missed more school than anyone I knew, spending many days propped up against pillows while I worked at sucking in enough air to keep from blacking out. By the time an attack ended, my arm and back muscles throbbed as if I'd worked out for hours.

> *My breath is corrupt, my days are extinct, the graves are ready for me.*
> JOB 17:1 KJV

I finally outgrew the asthma, and I thought I was done with it. Years later, however, it struck again, only more suddenly and harder somehow. Now, my family and I were in a time of adjustment, searching for medications to control the attacks and ease my breathing. There were shots and inhalers of various kinds, visits to the doctor, and experimenting to find the right medication for me.

Then there were the sudden, sharp attacks and times when the inhalers meant to open my lungs seemed to do just the opposite. There were times when the shots worked far too slowly or when the medications caused other serious side effects. Meanwhile, I struggled, full of fear and distress, not knowing if I'd even survive this frightening disease. Asthma doesn't have a cure, and many still die from it.

Alone in the darkest part of the night, not wanting to disturb my family every time I woke with my lungs tightening and fear wrenching my mind, I battled not just the disease but also the fear of that disease. Often, I wasn't sure I'd win. Often, I felt weak and helpless and desperate.

In those fearful struggles, each time an attack gripped me, I would silently cry out to God for his help, his comfort, and his soothing calm to ease my fears. He was always there, each time I sought him. I felt his presence as my breathing calmed and steadied again.

He got me through many long, sleepless, fear-filled nights until we found a balance of

In my distress I cried unto the Lord, and he heard me.
Psalm 120:1 KJV

medications to keep my breathing steady and my lungs open. Through those lonely, painful, frightening nights, God always heard my wordless, breathless cries, and he always helped me triumph over the pain and the fear of not being able to breathe.

PIERCING PAIN

How can you explain excruciating pain to someone who's never had it? The jolt of pain—it hurts to move, to think, to hear, to be. And what thankfulness when it's gone!

Dear God, the pain is so great and unbearable that I feel as though another moment of it will tear me apart. Please rescue me from this pain. Touch my body and heal me. Hear my pleas for only you have the power to deliver me from my affliction. Have mercy upon me. I cry out to you day and night, and I will turn to no one but you.

Lord, I am now in tribulation, and my heart is ill at ease, for I am much troubled with the present suffering.... Grant me patience, O Lord, even now in this moment. Help me, my God, and then I will not fear, how grievously soever I be afflicted.

THOMAS A KEMPIS, *THE IMITATION OF CHRIST*

SOMEBODY KNOWS

Nobody knows someone else's pain, how much she or he hurts, the depth and power of it. Nobody can know for sure. Nobody knows... except the Lord.

So Satan went out from the presence of the Lord, and inflicted loathsome sores on Job from the sole of his foot to the crown of his head. Job took a potsherd with which to scrape himself, and sat among the ashes.

Then his wife said to him, "Do you still persist in your integrity? Curse God, and die." But he said to her, "You speak as any foolish woman would speak. Shall we receive the good at the hand of God, and not receive the bad?" In all this Job did not sin with his lips...

> *Job was in great pain, yet he could say of God, "Though he slay me, yet will I trust in him."*
> Job 13:15 KJV.

And the Lord restored the fortunes of Job.... The Lord blessed the latter days of Job more than his beginning.

Job 2:7-10; 42:10, 12 NRSV

My brothers and sisters, whenever you face trials of any kind, consider it nothing but joy, because you know that the testing of your faith produces endurance; and let endurance have its full effect, so that you may be mature and complete, lacking in nothing.

JAMES 1:2-4 NRSV

THE PAINTING

It hangs on the wall and draws my gaze at night when the house is dark and still. A patient lies suffering on her sickbed, clearly in pain. Nurse and doctor hover nearby. But nearer still stands her Lord, one hand on her forehead to soothe away her pain. Some nights, I linger, staring hard at that painting, imagining myself there, in her place, soaking up comfort from my Lord.

SPARE ME?

I'd like to pray to be spared of all pain, but life is full of pain. No one escapes it. Better to ask God to be near whenever it comes.

Another valley of life is the aging process. One thing is certain: If we keep living, we are going to keep getting older. Getting older for many people is a depressing experience. It really is one of life's deepest valleys. But age should be one of life's greatest inspirations. Age can bring assurance, satisfaction, and peace of mind that nothing else can bring.

CHARLES L. ALLEN, *VICTORY IN THE VALLEYS OF LIFE*

WHAT I DO KNOW

I don't know which is worse, the wrenching physical pain or the emotional anguish with it. What I do know is that he will take care of all my hurts.

Fear old age, and old age can be a terrible experience.... There is power in fear. Power to torment. Power to snare your soul. Power to paralyze your potential, to render you ineffective, to handicap you in life.... Resist fear in Jesus' name.

DON GOSSETT, *LIVING WITH FEAR*

My heart is sore pained within me: and the terrors of death are fallen upon me. Fearfulness and trembling are come upon me, and horror hath overwhelmed me.

PSALM 55:4-5 KJV

I WILL NOT LEAVE YOU COMFORTLESS

In our worst moments, shattered by pain in body, mind, and spirit, God has promised not to leave us alone or without comfort.

Because the Lord is my Shepherd, I have everything I need! He lets me rest in the meadow grass and leads me beside the quiet streams. He gives me new strength. He helps me do what honors him the most. Even when walking through the dark valley of death I will not be afraid, for you are close beside me, guarding, guiding all the way.

PSALM 23:1-4 TLB

BIRTH PANGS

Part way through, she wants to stop, quit, and walk away. Enough of this tearing pain in her abdomen. But her body has other ideas, and from her pain comes a blessed new life—a beautiful new child.

I can rely on Him alone—for physical strength as for every other need.

CATHERINE MARSHALL, *A CLOSER WALK*

THANKFUL

Thank God when the pain ends, when once again we're well and whole and strong. Thank God when our bodies are released from the blinding, mind-numbing hurts that affect our whole lives. Thank God when we have complete victory over the pain.

TRAPPED IN HIS CAR

It was on all the TV stations, in newspapers and magazines all over the country—a man trapped inside his vehicle when the October 1989 earthquake collapsed one highway deck on top of another in Oakland, California. Confined in his crushed car for over three days, he was finally pulled out alive, a victory for rescuers who had struggled against discouragement. Nevertheless, he must have suffered terribly, for he died a few weeks later in the hospital.

Weeping may endure for a night, but joy cometh in the morning.

PSALM 30:5 KJV

Well-wishers all over the nation mourned his death, but his family and friends were thankful that he survived long enough to be rescued alive and did not have to die alone in his crushed vehicle. At least, the people who cared about him were able to share his final hours. God had given him those precious times, those last memories left behind for loved ones and for strangers who had heard his story.

Even though he lost his life, the story of his re-markable survival for so many days, his tough determination, the dramatic rescue efforts, and the faith of his family inspired people everywhere in their hardest moments—their times of pain, trouble, and discouragement—to place their trust in God.

My flesh and my heart may fail, but God is the strength of my heart and my portion forever.

PSALM 73:26 NRSV

But in the end, Jesus reminds us, the pain of earthly death is not the most important thing. What matters most is the eternal life that God has promised us. This is a gift that we can enjoy not just at the end of our earthly existence but begin-ning now, in the ways we live each day.

JIMMY CARTER, SOURCES OF STRENGTH

Out of Pain

The story went that he was in pain, constant pain, and from the center of all that hurt, they say he created wonderful music, bringing something truly good out of it.

Sometimes our faith delivers us from difficulties, and sometimes it delivers us in difficulties. Either way, God honors our faith and He gets the glory.…I'm inclined to believe that God can get greater glory at times by giving grace to live with our suffering than power to escape it.

WARREN W. WIERSBE, *WHY US? WHEN BAD THINGS HAPPEN TO GOD'S PEOPLE*

A Signal

Pain can be a signal, a reminder to reach out for help to others and to God. Let us always act on that signal.

Why is there so much pain in the world, God? It's so hard to understand. Lord, help us through it all. Help us comprehend or at least simply trust in you.

IN THE HOSPITAL

So much pain and misery all in one place. No wonder so many people avoid hospitals. Yet there are nurses, doctors, aids, volunteers, all those health workers who have committed their lives to ending pain and who are there for us all.

You and I do not have a thing to fear simply because we are growing older. If our faith is firmly fixed in the Savior, we can count on Him to be waiting at the end of the road to greet us. In fact, He'll be waiting up for us. Our room is all ready. The light is on. We are expected. He will welcome us home.

CHARLES R. SWINDOLL, *LIVING ON THE RAGGED EDGE*

Sometimes pain can burn so deep, scorching away at the center of self, bringing utter darkness and despair—yet even in this most terrible of pain, we can turn to you, Lord, for courage, comfort, strength, and the victory you so lovingly offer us, giving us light and hope to see us through.

I Cry Out

In the depth of my pain, I cry out to God. In grief and sorrow, in loss and anguish, I cry out to God. When I am overwhelmed and cannot bear another moment, I cry out to God. And He hears my cry. He listens and cares and answers, as He always has throughout all time.

Extending Mercy

The wreck was terrible. The boat was mangled beyond recognition. One young man was instantly killed, and another was severely injured. After the funeral for their lost friend, a group of teens waited and wondered whether their injured friend, James, would live or die. His head injuries were serious, and in those early days the outcome was uncertain.

Then came endless hours in a haze of pain, medication, and dazed confusion. He'd lost so much; his brain suffered such traumatic damage. His doctors

Therefore we do not lose heart. Though outwardly we are wasting away, yet inwardly we are being renewed day by day.

2 CORINTHIANS 4:16 NIV

couldn't guarantee he'd ever fully recover; he might never be the same. It would take months of rehabilitation and retraining for him to even begin tackling the simplest tasks. He must relearn how to talk, walk, and eat by himself.

As James groped for recovery, his friends came to see him, clearly uncomfortable and unsure what to say or do. Nevertheless, they came and encouraged him, letting him know that they cared about him. Yet his efforts to speak were as difficult to understand as the first words of a child, and James became frustrated and upset.

Adam, however, listened to James's every word, closely and carefully, until he could understand what James wanted to tell them. Though he'd never seemed the most patient or sensitive person before, Adam worked hard to help James. It was Adam who sat beside James, talking slowly and clearly, telling James all the latest news. It was Adam who brought small gifts and special treats. And it was Adam who made sure James still felt included in their group.

Adam didn't become impatient or discouraged when James struggled to find words or to remember their names. He reminded James of upcoming holidays and events. When James seemed down and discouraged, Adam patted his shoulder and kept his spirits up. When James seemed confused and uncertain, Adam helped calm his anxieties. Somehow Adam discovered an amazing gift of compassion within himself.

The rest of the group never knew how Adam was able to be so patient and strong for James, but Adam did. He had received a special gift from

God, an extra measure of strength and kindness to be able to help a friend through the hardest and most painful months of his life. Just as God was there for Adam, Adam was there for James, helping his friend to heal in body, mind, and spirit.

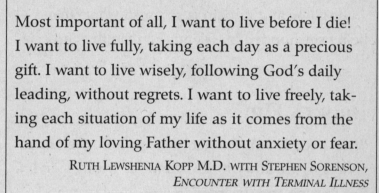

Most important of all, I want to live before I die! I want to live fully, taking each day as a precious gift. I want to live wisely, following God's daily leading, without regrets. I want to live freely, taking each situation of my life as it comes from the hand of my loving Father without anxiety or fear.

RUTH LEWSHENIA KOPP M.D. WITH STEPHEN SORENSON,
ENCOUNTER WITH TERMINAL ILLNESS

SPLINTER

Such a tiny sliver of wood to cause such sharp pain. Yet it reminds me to pray for those with far more serious hurts.

Lord, help them, comfort them and bring them peace and sweet, pain-free sleep. Ease the tension in their bodies and the ache in their hearts. Heal their hurts, please, Lord, and let them rest easy.

PAIN IS BETTER SHARED

To be alone and in pain is so much worse than being surrounded by friends and family who care.

BROKEN HIP

She'd been so full of energy, a dynamo, the one in charge of the household. Then one wrong step left her hurting and disabled in a hospital bed, and her whole life changed. Nevertheless, her heart was full of courage, and she could lean on us awhile as we had so often leaned on her.

Do not sit down baffled by your difficulties and infirmities, but turn from them to claim Christ's abundant grace and strength, that at the end of life you may have done all that was set you to do, and more, because the greatness of your need made you lean more heavily on His infinite resources.

F. B. Meyer, Our Daily Walk

Let Me

She can't fasten the buttons the way she used to. Her fingers are stiff and awkward. "Here, let me," I said, while thinking, "Someday younger hands will help me, too."

Watch Care

When Polly can't feed herself, Sam bends to help her. When she falters in mid-step, lost in her own mind, he guides her steps. When she weeps in confusion, in pain, or in fear, he comforts her and in caring for her finds easing of his own pain. In sickness and in health, Sam had vowed, and now he keeps his promise.

O, I have suffered
With those that I saw suffer.

WILLIAM SHAKESPEARE, *THE TEMPEST*

Lord, when it hurts too much to even pray, when pain overwhelms us, you are still here, close and caring.

ALZHEIMER'S

Does she feel pain over all she's lost—the memories and ideas, talents and skills? She's not the person she used to be and that brings her family pain, but they tend to her with such patient kindness, recalling all she's been and loving her all the more.

Look upon mine affliction and my pain.

PSALM 25:18 KJV

It's Just Old Age

He grimaces with a twinge of pain. "What is it? What's wrong?" his daughter asks.

"It's just old age," he tells her. The pain, she guesses, is as emotional as physical, and she rubs his neck to ease the pain by loving him and simply being there.

God, you understand it all. You know what we feel. You ache with us. After all, your Son died in pain–nailed to a cross.

Then the Lord said [to Moses], "I have observed the misery of my people who are in Egypt; I have heard their cry on account of their taskmasters. Indeed, I know their sufferings, and I have come down to deliver them from the Egyptians, and to bring them up out of that land to a good and broad land, a land flowing with milk and honey."

EXODUS 3:7-8 NRSV

OUR DELIVERER

Praise the Lord, for he has seen the affliction and heard the groans of his people—both his children who were slaves in Egypt and us who were in bondage to physical pain. Indeed, he has come to me in my darkest moment and rescued me from my misery. He is a compassionate and wonderful God, who loves his children and watches over each one of us.

Dear God, you have sustained me through my illness. You have nursed my injury. You are my true physician, and I glorify you with all my heart. Amen.

CHAPTER 6

MOVING ON

"FOR EVERYTHING there is a season," even for times of loss and of sorrow. The pain of losing someone dear to us or watching a relationship come to an end can be overwhelming. We feel bereft and alone, confused and lost, certain that we will hurt like this forever.

This is our darkest hour when we feel we cannot suffer any worse. Yet something inside whispers to us, "For everything there is a season," and we notice the faint glimmer of hope at the end of this long, dark tunnel of despair. The more we focus on the voice, the louder it becomes. The more we seek the light, the brighter it becomes. This is God's love and compassion for us making itself known, and in his growing presence, we become stronger and our faith is renewed.

STARTING OVER

Rachel was an expert at dealing with an alcoholic spouse. She had been married to Dan for 14 years, 12 of which were embroiled in the pain and conflict of coming to terms with his abusive behavior. When she had met him, Rachel had no idea how much drinking was a part of Dan's life. Over time, however, the pressures of married life and a growing family, along with increased responsibilities at work, had removed Dan's mask. The truth of his disease then became obvious.

Rachel had grown up in an alcoholic family herself, and like her mother, she had learned to be the perfect enabler. She knew how to lie for Dan and make excuses for his verbally abusive behavior, and even help get him drunk if it meant peace around the dinner table.

But after 14 years of trying unsuccessfully to help Dan get into treatment, she knew she was going to snap. With the responsibility of two growing boys, Rachel realized that she had to make a choice and either force Dan into treatment or leave the marriage to save herself and her children. She finally got up enough courage to give her husband, whom she truly loved and wanted to help, the ultimatum that she hoped would save his life and their relationship. But Dan wanted nothing to do with getting help, and he became even more abusive, this time actually hitting her one night in front of the boys.

Rachel knew that her choice had been made for her. She prayed for the fortitude to carry her through a long

Call on me in the day of trouble; I will deliver you, and you shall glorify me.

PSALM 50:15 NRSV

period of emotional and financial struggle, and with God and the support of her friends and family on her side, she left her dysfunctional marriage to start over.

The year ahead was one of extremes: relief and joy for having a new start on life; regret and anguish for the life she left behind. Dan continued to avoid treatment and rarely made any attempts to see her or the boys. Sadly, Rachel filed for divorce and full custody. When it was all over, she realized she should have left that destructive situation a long time ago. Now her life would be devoted to healing the damage Dan's drinking and her enabling had done to her sons, who were already showing signs of rage toward their father.

Blessed are those who trust in the Lord.
JEREMIAH 17:7 NRSV

Nevertheless, Rachel realized that although her marriage had ended, those years were not wasted ones but times of spiritual growth for her soul. Now she knew she had the strength and wisdom to no longer enable anyone, including herself, in such a disease. She had come through the fire, and God had purified her with his transforming love.

Every good thing that comes into our lives carries within it the power to make us fear its loss. Yet, at those distressing times when we lose our grip on the things we think will save us, there is something beyond the fear. It is the recognition that

loss can carry hope along with it: the hope that
what is taken away will be replaced by something
even better.

Joseph Biuso and Brian Newman, Receiving Love

**God of my heart, I am a broken person. I do not
know how to handle this suffering. I am not strong
enough to do it alone. Be my strength, God, and do
for me what I simply cannot do for myself. Be the
glue that binds the pieces of my shattered soul back
together, that I may rise and step back onto the
joyful path of life again. Amen.**

Connect With God

When we lose a spouse, we must take time to go
within and reaffirm our connection with God.
Once we are able to feel God's presence at work
in our lives, we will know that we already have all
we need to help us move beyond the grief and
begin to live and love again.

Out of sorrow the sweetest souls have emerged. The most sympathetic hearts are marked with scars from wounds which have healed.

LEROY BROWNLOW, *JESUS WEPT*

GETTING THROUGH

When a long-term relationship comes to an end, it's natural to mourn the loss of a companion and to grieve the death of a particular way of life. But we can mourn and grieve only for so long, then we must ask God to give us the grace and the courage to finally close that door and walk toward a new door waiting to be opened. We must take the next step God has for us.

Let go and let God see you through.
Give in and let God be with you.
Surrender to a love that heals all things.
Let go and let God be your wings.

Like the Water Lily

We can take a lesson from the precious water lily. For no matter what outside force or pressure is put upon the lily, it always rises back to the water's surface again to feel the nurturing sunlight upon its leaves and petals. We must be like the lily, steadfast and true in the face of every difficulty, that we too may rise above our problems and feel God's light upon our faces again.

Love the Lord with all your might;
Turn to him, seek him day and night[.]

WILLIAM WORDSWORTH, "PETER BELL"

Unbreakable Strength

The resilient heart withstands the winds of change, just as the flexible branch of a tree bends but does not break.

Death is not the only reason for grief. There are as many kinds of losses as there are people and no two are alike....God is dependable in grief always—no matter what causes it.

EUGENIA PRICE, *GETTING THROUGH THE NIGHT*

THE FAITH TO CLIMB MOUNTAINS

If we have but faith the size of a mustard seed, we can ascend this mountain of suffering and descend into the valley of serenity, which is on the other side.

Lord, you are the light I follow down this long, dark tunnel. You are the voice that whispers, urging me onward when this wall of sorrow seems insurmountable. You are the hand that reaches out and grabs mine when I feel like I am sinking in despair. You alone, Lord, are the waters that fill me when I am dried up of all hope and faith. I thank you, Lord, for although I may feel like giving up, you have not given up on me. Amen.

If you have lost a spouse through death or divorce, Jesus knows and understands. He will weep with you as you go through this valley of loss. He will sit with you until the sorrow is bearable, until the ache lessens.

JAN McCRAY, *THE LOVE EVERY WOMAN NEEDS*

A Brighter Tomorrow

For just as the harshest winter always gives way to the warm blush of spring, the season of our suffering will give way to a brighter tomorrow, where change becomes a catalyst for new growth and spiritual maturity, and we are able to move on with the joyfulness of being alive.

There is a future for you, a future filled with hope…if you put your past and your future into Jesus Christ's care, you can discover, as others have, His capacity to create from your pain beauty and joy and completeness.

MAUREEN RANK, *FREE TO GRIEVE*

Miracles Come in Twos

Jennie thought this had to be the best day of her life. Not only had she and her husband, Rich, just learned that she was pregnant but that twins were on the way. Because they had been trying to conceive for years and had run into countless health-related obstacles, they thought it would never happen, but the proof was in the ultrasound image they took home from the doctor's office.

Four months into the pregnancy, Jennie experienced unusual cramping and spotting, and she had to be rushed to the emergency room late one night. The doctor on duty attended to Jennie with a calm and professional precision, making her as comfortable as possible before quietly telling her that she was in an extremely delicate situation. Jennie panicked, grabbing Rich's hand for support while the doctor continued to examine her. When the doctor put the stethoscope on Jennie's stomach, the look on her face was tight and unreadable, but Jennie could sense that something was terribly wrong. Her intuition was confirmed when additional tests showed the fetuses had died in the womb.

For over a month, Rich did what he could to comfort Jennie, but she was inconsolable. She had given the twins names and continued to speak into her tummy as if they were still alive. She simply could not, would not accept, that she would not have children.

Do not be grieved, for the joy of the Lord is your strength.

NEHEMIAH 8:10 NRSV

As the strain of Jennie's grief and his own sadness took its toll on Rich, he realized he would have to be the stronger one at this dark time. He knew that if he could not help Jennie cope, she might never recover from her mourning. Lying in bed at night, he prayed for direction as he watched his wife toss and turn from a sedative-induced sleep. He prayed that the right answer would soon come and that his wife would be able to move through her suffering and accept the loss of their twins.

As the days went on, no big miracles occurred, but Rich could definitely see that Jennie was getting stronger. She used the sleeping sedatives less, she started eating better, and she even began to do one of her favorite hobbies before the loss—jigsaw puzzles. It calmed her, and Rich was thrilled when she came to him one day and put her arms around him. It was the first sign of affection he had felt from her in a long time.

To every thing there is a season, and a time to every purpose under the heaven.

ECCLESIASTES 3:1 KJV

Jennie finally came to accept the loss of the twins, and even of any possibility of giving birth. Her doctor confirmed she would never be able to bring a child to full term. Yet what proved to Rich that God's grace was indeed flowing in their lives was the morning Jennie asked him to sit down and discuss the possibility of adoption. The glow in her eyes when she talked about loving and caring for a child that no one else wanted assured Rich that everything was going to be all right. When they eventually went into the adoption agency for an interview, the woman who assisted them told them they would have no trouble at all, as they were a loving and stable couple.

Four months later, Jennie and Rich brought home not one, but two beautiful baby girls whose mother and father had been killed in a plane crash. They were given the very same names that Jennie had once hoped to give her own twins, Hope and Faith, and they were loved just as much as if they had indeed been born from Jennie's womb. As Rich watched Jennie mother and fuss over their new girls, he knew in his heart that God not only had heard his prayers but also had provided them with a miracle.

Make that two miracles!

Praise be to the God and Father of our Lord Jesus Christ, the Father of compassion and the God of all comfort, who comforts us in all our troubles, so that we can comfort those in any trouble with the comfort we ourselves have received from God.

2 CORINTHIANS 1:3-4 NIV

When we have experienced a devastating loss, His aim is not simply to put something in its place. His aim is to minister to the hurting soul. If I lose a child, I might be helped by receiving another child—but I am not healed. Our infinitely wise God does far more than replace.... He's trying to reach your heart and heal you, but He requires your cooperation.

BETH MOORE, *WHISPERS OF HOPE*

God, I know that you close some doors in my life in order to open new ones. I know that things change and come to an end in order to leave room for new beginnings. Help me have the boldness and enthusiasm to let go of the old and accept the new. Amen.

Jim voiced a prayer. "Lord, You know how we feel. The forces of evil would like to torment us with guilt and depression. I pray that You would over-rule and bless us with a night of rest, which we so desperately need. Thank You, Father, for loving us. In Jesus' name, amen."

God answered our prayer. We awakened refreshed and sought help in planning a memorial service that would be a celebration of life—not an anguishing over death.

FRAN CAFFEY SANDIN, *SEE YOU LATER JEFFREY*

GET UP, GET OVER, GET ON

When the despair that comes with the pain of a loss immobilizes us and makes us feel powerless, God gives us the inner fortitude and grace we need to get up, get over the suffering, and get on with our lives.

Dark days do not last forever. The clouds are always moving, though very slowly. The person in the midst of depression is certain, of course, that the clouds are not moving.... One of the most helpful things we can do for a friend at such a time is to stand by that friend in quiet confidence, and assure him or her that this, too, shall pass.

GRANGER E. WESTBERG, *GOOD GRIEF*

Silver Linings

Just as each cloud is lined with silver, so, too, is each painful experience lined with the miracle of lessons learned and wisdom gained. God never takes something from us without giving us something else in return.

Use the gift of listening....Listening is hard. The sound of our own voices may be therapy for us, but it is not necessarily healing for the wounded griever. During a time of shock people need to repeat their story over and over again. You may think they would grow weary of giving details, or telling what happened, but that isn't the case at all.

BILLY GRAHAM, *FACING DEATH AND THE LIFE AFTER*

There's Always Tomorrow

God of my heart, bring me comfort and peace in this time of confusion and sorrow. Help me know that although things are bleak, there is always a brighter tomorrow.

From my own tears I have learned that if you follow your tears, you will find your heart. If you find your heart, you will find what is dear to God. And if you find what is dear to God, you will find the answer to how you should live your life.

KEN GIRE, *WINDOWS OF THE SOUL*

When the anguish of loss overwhelms us,
and we feel there's no reason to live.
We must look deep within to find meaning
and to know we've still so much to give.

FILLING THE VOID WITH GOD

Traumatic events leave a void in our souls that only a closer relationship with God can fill. By asking God to help us through hard times, we truly come to understand that we are never alone and that sadness is only a precursor to joy and pain a precursor to healing.

When we are helpless and without relief or are devoid of comfort, God is most willing to aid and comfort us.

E. M. BOUNDS, *OBTAINING ANSWERS TO PRAYER*

STEPPING STONES

Life's tragedies make us into stepping stones. Without suffering, we would be like lumps of clay that have not yet been fired in the potter's oven to a transforming state of usefulness.

I, too, have learned some lessons. I have learned that nothing belongs to me—not Debbie, not all my other loved ones, not my material possessions. Even my own life belongs to God. He has merely let me enjoy them for a season.

DALE EVANS ROGERS, *DEAREST DEBBIE*

NEVER TOO LATE FOR LAUGHTER

From the time he could talk, Jordan made people laugh, and all through his teenage years, he had the wonderful ability to bring humor into every situation. Yet, when he announced to his father, a staunchly conservative financial advisor, that stand-up comedy was his career goal, Jordan knew their relationship would never be the same.

To Jordan, it seemed that his father had always talked at him about his need to find a good moneymaking career or about how well off other people Jordan's age were doing. Although his father never told Jordan he should not be a stand-up comedian, his actions made it quite clear it was not a choice his father approved of.

God has brought laughter for me; everyone who hears will laugh with me.
GENESIS 21:6 NRSV

Over the years, Jordan traveled the tumultuous road of doing stand-up in any bar, club, or alley corner that would book him. He made little money at first, but he loved it. When he turned to his father for financial assistance during a particularly dry spell, Jordan received a lecture on how stupid his dreams were and how he should "shape up" and be like other people, working hard for a living at something with a future. Jordan lashed out at his father, and the words between them became harsh and cold. That was the last time Jordan ever spoke to his father.

Jordan was tired of always feeling like a failure in his father's eyes. It didn't matter

He has made everything beautiful in its time.

ECCLESIASTES 3:11 NIV

that comedy made Jordan happy; that was not important to his father. What was important was "making a living" and not "making a life." Jordan knew that if he was ever going to keep his confidence, he could not be around someone who did not believe in him, even if it was his father.

Three years later, Jordan's hard work and passion finally paid off. He was headlining shows, and he had even been offered a lead role in a TV sitcom. But the true payoff came when he was booked to play the famous Comedy Store in Los Angeles to a standing-room-only crowd, which was taped for TV broadcast. The excitement was short-lived, however, when Jordan received a phone call from his mother telling him his father had passed away the night before of massive coronary failure.

Jordan took the first plane out. All the way there, his gut was tight with regrets; regrets for not having been there to say goodbye, and mostly regrets that his father never saw him living his dreams. When he arrived at his mother's house, she embraced him for a long, long time. They made funeral arrangements right away, and the burial took place that weekend. Jordan felt like the prodigal son who came home, but too late for reconciliation. As he watched his father's body lowered into the ground, he felt the heavy weight of the past three years bear down on him like a ton of bricks.

That evening, Jordan got a chance to talk with his mother, and he poured out his heart and soul to her. He told her how much he had resented his father's lack of belief in his dreams, and how much he had desperately wanted to share his success with his father.

Jordan's mother got up, went to a storage trunk, and took out a large photo album. She placed it on Jordan's lap and whispered, "You were his hero, Jordan." Jordan opened the book to find page after page of newspaper and magazine clippings about his rise to fame as a comedy star. He couldn't believe his eyes. "He watched you on TV last night, and he really wanted us to fly out and see the show, but he had been feeling ill," she told her son.

"He was your biggest fan," she continued. "He used to be afraid for you, that this dream would break your heart. When he saw how you plowed ahead and became a success, it made him the happiest man alive. He wanted to call you many times, but he didn't. He was afraid of what you'd say. But he loved you, and he loved the way you could make him laugh so hard his heart ached."

Jordan went to his father's grave the next morning. He sat in silence for a long time, weeping over the fact that he could never make things right in this life. As he sat there, a feeling of God's peace flowed over him like morning sunlight, and Jordan knew that it was never too late to make things right. He stood up, brushed the dirt off his pants, and right there at his father's grave,

> *Then you will know the truth, and the truth will set you free.*
> JOHN 8:32 NIV

performed an entire ad-libbed stand-up routine about love, death, forgiveness, letting go, and coming back home again.

He knew in his heart that somewhere his father was laughing.

God, bless this situation with the gentle, healing power of your love, that I may find the courage to carry on through this dark time of loss and the grace to believe that there is happiness ahead. Amen.

ETERNALLY YOURS

If you have suffered the loss of someone you love, remember that although his or her body has gone from this earth, the love you shared remains an eternal and joyful presence in your life. Indeed, they will be eternally yours.

What will you do when the message of death comes to you? Will you have Christ in your heart with the grace to stand the loss? Will there be a hope in your breast of seeing your loved one again?

DALLAS BILLINGTON, *GOD IS REAL*

John Newton looked at his dear friends who were gathered around his bed. When he saw the tears in their eyes and the sadness on their faces he said, "Why should you all be so sad? Don't you realize that when I shut my eyes on this world for the last time I will open them to a far better one?

What a wonderful thing it is to live under the shadow of the protective wings of the Almighty God."

Kay Marshall Strom, John Newton: The Angry Sailor

In times of loss and sorrow,
when hearts are dark with pain,
we find a source of light within
to make life bright again.

And now the congregation began singing. Fanny smiled amid her tears. It's one thing to write about God's promises; it's quite another to re-member those promises when you need them! Grief? Yes, she would sorrow a long time over the loss of her friend. But even as she mourned she would enjoy the sure knowledge that separation is temporary.

Sandra Dengler, Fanny Crosby—Writer of 8000 Songs

THE MYSTERY OF THE ETERNAL

The passing of a dear one often leaves us wondering "Why, God, why?" If we knew that death is the beginning of a new mystery, a new adventure to unfold, we would feel joy for those who leave this earth and joy for those yet to leave.

Our society instills in us the belief that death is the end that is to be dreaded. God tells us this is not true. He never promised that while on earth we would have a rose garden, but He has promised that our greatest blessings will come after we die.

HERM WEISKOPF, *HIS FIVE SMOOTH STONES*

Dear God, help me know that the bond between this person who has passed away and me is an eternal bond. Teach me to understand that what may appear to be a "good-bye" is really only an "until we meet again." Amen.

Life is real! Life is earnest!
And the grave is not its goal;
Dust thou art, to dust returnest;
Was not spoken of the soul.

HENRY WADSWORTH LONGFELLOW, "A PSALM OF LIFE"

For the believer, death is a transition, not a termination.

LESLIE B. FLYNN, THE SUSTAINING POWER OF HOPE

LIFT UP YOUR HEARTS

Lift up your heart in sweet surrender to the God who is waiting to shower you with blessings. Lift up your soul on wings of joy to the God who is waiting to guide you from the chaos and shadows out into the light of a peace that knows no equal.

But in the meantime, God is able to use our suffering to glorify Himself. It is not wasted!

JONI EARECKSON TADA, GLORIOUS INTRUDER

Do not let your hearts be troubled. Believe in God, believe also in me. In my Father's house there are many dwelling places. If it were not so, would I have told you that I go to prepare a place for you? And if I go and prepare a place for you, I will come again and will take you to myself, so that where I am, there you may be also.

JOHN 14:1-4 NRSV

Dear God, some of the greatest lessons we learn are only after our hearts have suffered. For in times of pain we receive wisdom, and in times of sorrow we gain understanding. This is your way of teaching our hearts that we must know darkness in order to embrace your light. Thank you for being our compassionate teacher. Amen.

BEYOND SORROW

When the loss of someone we dearly love brings a cold darkness to our lives, it seems that darkness will be forever with us and our hearts will never feel joy again. We believe then that night will never end and day will never come. Yet the darkness will leave and the night will end when we hold on to our Lord, for he will bring light back into our lives. And in that light, our hopes will be renewed and a joy will reside in our hearts once again.

The Lord is near to all who call on him, to all who call on him in truth. He fulfills the desire of all who fear him; he also hears their cry, and saves them. The Lord watches over all who love him.

PSALM 145:18-20

We praise you, Lord, for eternal life. And we thank you for your love for each one of us. Amen.

CHAPTER 7

WHEN GOD SEEMS FAR AWAY

ALONG WITH LIFE'S blessings, there are also struggles, pain, and loss. While we never welcome these things, we all must go through them. At such times we most keenly feel our need for intervention, and we call out to God.

But what if no answer comes and it seems as if God himself has forgotten us? What if our faith in him is shaken to its very core, and still he is silent? Interestingly, the Bible is full of such themes: men and women of faith crying out to God from their deeply troubled souls. Even Jesus, while he died, called out to his Father, asking why he had forsaken him. This chapter seeks to offer a foothold of assurance that, in those times when it seems God is far away, in reality, he is holding us close to his heart.

HAVE YOU GIVEN UP ON ME, GOD?

Carolyn's situation was becoming increasingly desperate. Each morning she would wake with a feeling of anxiety. A teacher of third graders, Carolyn loved her work, but lately, getting up in front of her class felt like climbing an emotional Mount Everest. At times, a sense of panic and shortness of breath would grip her. It took every fiber of self-control she could muster to keep from bursting into tears whenever an attack occurred. "God, what is happening to me? Please help me get this under control!" she prayed repeatedly.

"Fear and trembling overwhelms me."
PSALM 55:5 NRSV

Carolyn's friends knew her as a calm, stable, even-tempered person, rarely expressing extreme emotion. However, Carolyn knew she was becoming an emotional basket case. This was particularly evident when Carolyn was invited to a special dinner party in the home of some friends. Even though she had felt apprehensive about going, Carolyn was determined not to let her problem control her. Again she prayed, "God, please keep me from falling apart. I need your strength to make it through without breaking down."

"But I call upon God, and the Lord will save me."
Psalm 55:16 NRSV

At the party, Carolyn struggled to make conversation, and in the middle of dinner, Carolyn's heart began to race. The now-familiar choking sensation rendered her unable to swallow or speak. Tears filled her eyes. Getting up quickly from the table, Carolyn retreated to the washroom. "O God! Why did this have to happen here? How do I explain? I can't live like this? Where are you, God? Tell me what to do!"

Carolyn knew it was time to visit her doctor to see if this was something that could be treated. She did some research and thought perhaps she had symptoms of what are commonly referred to as "panic attacks," treatable with certain medications.

After several appointments and tests, Carolyn's suspicions were confirmed, and she began to take two kinds of medicine to treat her painful condition.

"I don't want to have to rely on drugs," Carolyn lamented to Melanie, a friend.

"But Carolyn, you likely won't have to take them forever. It probably will be just until things get leveled out again in your system."

Carolyn sighed. "I keep asking God to help me, but he doesn't seem to be listening. I'm really discouraged."

"Maybe God wants to give you the help you need through the wisdom and expertise of a doctor."

"I guess I was hoping for something more miraculous and less humiliating. It's embarrassing to have to take pills to cope with life."

"Carolyn! There's nothing to be ashamed of. I really think this is a delayed reaction from all the stress in the last several years. Now that things have let up and you're relaxing, your emotions are letting loose. You're only human, and you can't carry things inside forever."

"I know. But I feel as if God is disappointed in me and doesn't want to help."

"I don't think that's true at all, Carolyn. God has given you a safe place to land while you deal with this. You have friends all around you who care about you."

"I guess I hadn't seen it that way. I've wanted so much just to be healthy. I thought because I was sick, God had turned his back on me."

"Well, I'm not saying that having a health problem is easy, but given all the evidence, I can't help believing that God cares very much about you."

"Thanks, Melanie. I really need that reassurance right now."

If I count the things I've asked for that you have not given me, I begin to believe you do not love me,

God. But if, instead, I bring to mind all of the goodness you have shown me, I come to trust that you have never given me less than what I need and often have blessed me with far more from a depth of love I cannot comprehend.

DIFFERENCE, NOT INDIFFERENCE

Just because God's way of helping us is different than we hoped or expected, it doesn't mean he is indifferent to our cries for help. We must believe that he knows what is truly best for us and is actively doing what is best for us.

Ours is not a cosmic God who is powerful and holy, but indifferent. He knows when we hurt, where we are weak, and how we are tempted. Jesus is not only our Savior, but our loving Lord who sympathizes with us. Rejoice in the greatness of His love for us.

JOHN F. MACARTHUR, JR., *DRAWING NEAR*

HELP!

I prayed but got no answer,
I believed but nothing changed,
I waited and grew anxious,
God, help my failing faith!

Our enemy and God's is always busily at work distorting our vision, throwing confusion into our minds lest we see the glory that God is waiting to show us in everything that makes up our lives— the people we love, our homes, our work, our sufferings.

ELISABETH ELLIOT, *THE LIFE AND LEGACY OF AMY CARMICHAEL*

GOD'S HEARTBEAT

In the silence of despair, we hear nothing but the lonely beating of our own heart. In the silence of faith, however, rhythms of the world around us remind us that God's heart beats nearby.

These troubles and sufferings of ours are, after all, quite small and won't last very long. Yet this short time of distress will result in God's richest blessing upon us forever and ever! So we do not look at what we can see right now, the troubles all around us, but we look forward to the joys of heaven which we have not yet seen. The troubles will soon be over, but the joys to come will last forever.

2 CORINTHIANS 4:17-18 TLB

We would know, O God our Father, that Thou art near us and beside us; that Thou dost love us and that Thou art concerned about all our affairs. May we become aware of Thy companionship, of Him who walks beside us....O Lord Jesus, help us to know that when we reach up to Thee, Thou art reaching down to us. We ask in the name of Jesus, our Lord, AMEN.

CATHERINE MARSHALL, A MAN CALLED PETER

UNDERSTANDING IN ACTION

The best listeners are often silent, the depth of their understanding revealed by their actions. God is one such listener.

Dear God, waiting for you is the hardest part of life. Not knowing. Not understanding. Not being able to figure things out. And when you don't provide answers right away, I feel as if I'll go crazy. But when I stop a moment and think about it, it makes sense that there will be times when you ask me to just trust you, when you'll challenge my rhetoric about believing in you and teach me to be patient. So here I am. I'll be still and wait for you.

GOD, HAVE YOU LEFT ME ALONE?

Anthony's life wasn't perfect, but then, whose is? Actually, despite some rough edges, things were going quite well. His small-scale clothing business was steadily growing, he had just purchased a nice home, he was married to a wonderful woman, and the future looked promising.

With his life moving in a generally positive direction, Anthony just wasn't prepared for what happened next. Not realizing that the many hours he was having to invest in keeping his business running was causing his wife to be disenchanted with their relationship, Anthony was devastated when she told him she wanted a divorce. Try as he might to persuade her to stay and work on their problems, she had made up her mind. With his marriage suddenly and unexpectedly over, Anthony plummeted into despair, and the loneliness he felt was unbearable.

Anthony hadn't been a person who prayed a lot, but he did believe in God, and he tried to ease his loneliness by talking with God. His prayers, however, seemed to reach no higher than the ceiling of his now-empty home. He kept asking if God had left him alone, too? He felt abandoned, and he believed he had no one if God wasn't there.

The clothing business—the thing that had been instrumental in destroying his marriage—now became Anthony's saving grace. It was the one thing that kept him going through the motions of life when he felt as if he would rather just lock himself away and hide. And it was through the business that he met Marge and Joan—two seam-stresses with whom he contracted to repair some of the "seconds" he had purchased to sell in his store.

Early in the week, Anthony would drop off boxes of clothing at the women's shop, and

> *The Lord is near to all who call on him, to all who call on him in truth.*
> PSALM 145:18 NRSV

they would invite him to stay for a cup of tea. Anthony found himself enjoying their company, and his aching soul received a bit of comfort as new friendships emerged.

To his delight, Anthony discovered that he and Marge shared a common interest: Both played keyboards in a band. The two would talk about music styles, musicians, and songs they knew and loved. Marge would loan Anthony CDs of popular contemporary inspirational artists, and Anthony found that their music uplifted his heart and mind.

Meanwhile, a place of worship that Joan attended had a band that was looking for a keyboard player. She mentioned the position to Anthony, and he looked into it, showed up for some rehearsals, and ended up being just the person for the job.

Today, Anthony is convinced that it was no mistake that his need for meaningful relationships in his life led him to Joan and Marge. For it was through these two women that Anthony has become connected with a caring church community. Relationships he has built there have helped fill the vacancy in his heart, and through community with people of faith, Anthony has rediscovered the faith of his youth—a vibrant, relevant relationship with God.

"I had never been so alone in my life as when my wife left me," Anthony said, "but I've also never been more fulfilled in my relationships as I am now that God has become the key player in my life. I only wish I had known earlier how much his presence makes a difference in the relationships I have with other people. But while I can't change what's past, this I am sure of: God will never abandon me, and he can bring healing to a lonely heart."

Lord, you have seen each time when I've been abandoned by those in whose love I have trusted. You have known the loneliness in my soul. I must confess to you that it causes me to wonder if your love has failed me, too. I need you to assure me that you are still here and that you will always stay with me.

The First Move

Sometimes we must be the first to reach out to let others know we are willing to let their love in.

Right now, wherever you are, you can turn around and He'll be there *welcoming you*. Waiting to prove His love to you.

ETHEL WATERS, *TO ME IT'S WONDERFUL*

A Risk Worth Taking

The sting of rejection lingers long after it has been inflicted. It often creates an aversion to drawing near to the very thing that can bring healing: love through relationship with God and others. It takes a certain willingness to risk reaching out if we ever hope to find wholeness again. But there is no more worthwhile risk than that which risks for the sake of love.

The chief end of man is to glorify God. And it is more true in suffering than anywhere else that *God is most glorified in us when we are most satisfied in him.*

JOHN PIPER, *DESIRING GOD*

God's Wise Plan for Community

The Bible reveals that God promotes and values a healthy, caring community. When we invest ourselves in being a part of such a community, we will have others to pick us up and help us along when we have difficulty in our individual relationships with those closest to us.

But well for him whose feet hath trod
  The weary road of toil and strife,
  Yet from the sorrows of his life
Builds ladders to be nearer God.

OSCAR WILDE, "A LAMENT"

God, we know that pain has produced some wisdom in our lives, but it has also created cynicism and fear. People burn us, reject us, hurt us, and none of us wants to play the fool more than once, so we're tempted to close off our hearts to people and you. But relationships that bring meaning and joy require vulnerability. Help us trust you to be our truest friend and to lead us to the kind of community that will bring healing rather than destruction.

The steadfast love of the Lord never ceases,
his mercies never come to an end;
they are new every morning;
great is your faithfulness.
"The Lord is my portion," says my soul,
"therefore I will hope in him."

LAMENTATIONS 3:22-24 NRSV

THE LONELIEST NUMBER

The words *alone*, *lonely*, and *abandoned* all contain the word one. When we believe we stand by ourselves to face life's difficulties—just one person against the world—we will often feel alone, lonely, and abandoned. But in the words *community*, *fellowship*, and *family*, there is no longer the possibility that *one* might be left to stand alone.

Love the Lord your God, and love one another. Love one another as he loves. Love with strength and purpose and passion and no matter what comes against you. Don't weaken. Stand against the darkness and love. That's the way back into Eden. That's the way back to life.

Francine Rivers, *Redeeming Love*

Where Was God When Brian Died?

It was a quiet Sunday afternoon. The Fields family had been to church earlier that morning, and after arriving home, the day had been spent in a leisurely fashion—the children playing with friends, and Tanya and Jon catching up on little things around the house.

Ten-year-old Brian was roughhousing with his neighborhood buddy Shane. They played bucking broncos until the two were worn out and dinner-time was approaching. It was time for Shane to return home, so the boys said their goodbyes and Shane left.

A pillow (which had served as a saddle) still strapped to his back, Brian ambled into the kitchen. Tanya was talking with Jon as he made dinner preparations. Tanya smiled at their son and told him that dinner would be ready in 20 minutes. "That's enough time for you to get your room cleaned up, right?"

In an air of exaggerated defeat, the good-natured Brian lumbered out of the kitchen and down

> *O Lord, how long shall I cry for help, and you will not listen?*
>
> HABAKKUK 1:2

the hallway to his bedroom, closing the door behind him. Tanya went to work, straightening up rooms in the house where the boys had knocked things out of kilter. When dinner was close to being served, Tanya went to see how Brian was coming along on his cleanup project.

Opening the door, Tanya looked in to see her son slumped at the foot of his bed. She rushed over to him and laid him back on the floor to discover the belt that had been around his waist, holding the pillow in place, was now buckled tightly around his neck. With trembling hands she worked to free the buckle's catch from its notch as she shouted to Jon to call 911 immediately.

Tanya began CPR, crying out to God to help her save her son. Minutes later a sheriff arrived on the scene, followed by paramedics. All attempts to revive Brian failed. At the hospital, Jon and Tanya stood near Brian's body as they listened in disbelief: "We're terribly sorry; your son is dead."

In the week that followed, a flurry of activity carried the couple along as they contacted friends and relatives and made funeral arrangements. But once the immediate demands of their situation subsided, the agonizing truth remained: Their dear son was gone and would never be coming back to them.

The questions welled up in their souls; there was no holding them back. Where was God when Brian died? Was he looking the other way when the belt buckle locked into place, too tight for Brian to cry out? Was God tending to something else when Jon and Tanya had called out to him to help them save their only son?

God, where were you when Brian died? We wish you would tell us. You seem to have gone so far away. Can it be that you are uncaring—even cruel? We are devastated, and you are silent.

In the dark emptiness of Jon and Tanya's bereavement, time seemed to have become suspended and irrelevant. And whether a moment or an eternity was passing, it did not matter. Silence and sadness were cold, motionless statues that stared out from within their souls at the surreal quality the outside world had taken on. Many weary days passed and turned into dreary weeks. Grief ebbed and flowed, but always remained.

In their separate experiences, however, as they grappled with pain, Tanya and Jon each began to sense that something gentle was stealing into their hearts. It was an almost imperceptible whispering into the stony silence, a warm breath, full of peace and comfort:

"Your son is with me. I have taken him home."

God, is that you? Where have you been?

"I have been holding you—holding you close to my heart. 'There is a time to keep silent, and a time to speak.' Your soul could not bear my words until now, so I kept silent. But the time to speak has come."

Our son! Our son is dead!

"Oh, my dear children, my heart aches for you, for I know your pain. My Son also tasted death, but because he lives again, your son lives, too. This is the assurance of hope you may rest in."

Hope. Hope has all but left us, God. Where were you when we needed you?

> *Draw near to God, and he will draw near to you.*
> JAMES 4:8 NRSV

"I have been with you. I have never left your side. When it was time for Brian to come home, he took my hand, and we made the journey together. Now you must take my hand and let my grace sustain you, for I know it is sorrowful to go on without him."

God, why? Why did you take him from us?

"For each soul, there is a time to be born, and a time to die. Eternity will reveal what you cannot understand now. Trust my wisdom, and in time, I will lead you home, where Brian joyfully waits for you."

Help us, God! It is too much for us to bear. We need you to help us through.

"Come, I will carry you until you are strong again. Then, as a shepherd leads his sheep, I will lead you safely home."

How long, O Lord? Will you forget me forever?
How long will you hide your face from me?
How long must I bear pain in my soul,
and have sorrow in my heart all day long?
How long shall my enemy be exalted over me?

PSALM 13:1-2 NRSV

We are so limited in our perspective, God. We know you see things from an eternal viewpoint and that you ask us to trust that you are wise and loving. But when everything around us and within us seems to cry out that you are cruel and unjust,

**please hold steady our faith in your unfailing good-
ness. Amen.**

CONSOLING LOVE

Our loss touches God's heart deeply. He created
the one for whom we grieve, and he knows very
well the irreplaceable nature of the relationship
we shared. God does not minimize or misunder-
stand our pain. He weeps with us and longs to
console us with his love.

The heavens declare your glory, the whole world
is witness to your wonders. I find you in nature,
in birth and death and the very pain that is my
lot. All beauty speaks to me of you, all the creative arts. And I can speak to you through prayer;
your own Holy Spirit responds. Yet one thing
more I must have truly to be one with you. And
that is love.

MARJORIE HOLMES, *HOW CAN I FIND YOU, GOD?*

God's Gentle Power

The God who hung the stars in space will turn
  your darkness into light.
The God whose birds rise on the winds will give
  your injured soul new flight.
The God who taught the whale its song will cause
  your heart to sing again.
For the God whose power made earth and sky
  will touch you with his gentle hand.

As the one perfect, loving Father, He welcomes
our coming to Him—even spilling out our tears,
our sorrow, or our heartache. Bring it all into His
presence. He not only will accept your heart cry,
He will comfort you.

JACK HAYFORD, *I'LL HOLD YOU IN HEAVEN*

Truth or Circumstances?

No one knows the mind of God, nor why he
chooses to work the way he does. But in our most

difficult circumstances, we will miss the peace of his presence unless we persevere in trusting that he is always faithful and always good.

My grief feels as if it will never subside, God. Everything within me melts like wax when I wake up in the morning and realize all over again what has happened. My life is forever changed. Sometimes I wonder if you are there, but I know you have promised always to be with me. Please hold me close. Amen.

GOD'S TIMING

I was angry at my parents one day when I found a tennis racket for 25 cents at a second-hand store, and they would not let me buy it. "But I have the money! Why not?" I begged, my eyes clouding with tears.

"We don't want you spending your money on it right now" was all they would say. I knew that pressing the issue was not wise and pouting just wasn't permitted. So, I prudently regained my composure. Inside, however, I was seething: *They're so mean!*

A few weeks later, I celebrated my eleventh birthday, and after blowing out my birthday candles, I unwrapped a beautiful aluminum racket, a far better model than the warped wooden one I had coveted at the thrift store.

I can't help but think that I often unfairly despise God as I had despised my parents that day long ago. He truly has my best interests at heart. I just have to learn to wait for his perfect timing to be able to enjoy the blessings he has in store.

You have something eternally precious in common with Christ—suffering!

JONI EARECKSON TADA & STEVEN ESTES, *WHEN GOD WEEPS*

See, the home of God is among mortals.
He will dwell with them;

they will be his peoples,
and God himself will be with them;
he will wipe every tear from their eyes.
Death will be no more;
mourning and crying and pain will be no more,
for the first things have passed away.

REVELATION 21:3-4 NRSV

Thank you Lord for helping us through our hard times. You have shown us your love for us and made us more compassionate people. Help us to show the same love to others who are going through hard times.

Original inspirations written by:

Christine A. Dallman is a freelance writer, who has contributed to the devotional publication *The Quiet Hour* and is a former editor and columnist for *Sunday Digest* magazine. She is the author of *Daily Devotions for Seniors*, an inspirational resource for maturing adults.

Marie D. Jones is widely published in both books and magazines and has contributed to titles that include *The Silver Book of Hope* and *Bless This Marriage*.

Karen M. Leet is a writer whose work has appeared in numerous regional, family, juvenile, and inspirational publications. She has contributed to various books, including *Silver Linings: Friends* and *She Who Laughs, Lasts*.

Barbara Roberts Pine is an author and speaker who has lectured at religious retreats and leadership seminars, and her published writing includes the book *Life with a Capital "L"*.

Other quotations compiled by **Elaine Creasman.**

Publications International, Ltd., has made every effort to locate the owners of all copyrighted material to obtain permission to use the selections that appear in this book. Any errors or omissions are unintentional; corrections, if necessary, will be made in future editions.

Page 29: From "God of Grace and God of Glory" by Harry Emerson Fosdick. Copyright ©1954. Used by permission of Brodt Music Company, Inc.

Page 101: From *A Touch of His Love* by Charles Stanley. Copyright ©1994. Used by permission of Zondervan Publishing House.

Page 103: Taken from *In Times of Pain* by Jane Grayshon. Copyright ©1990. Published by Lion Publishing and reproduced by permission.

Page 107: From "Keep Me Faithful" by Ruth Harms Calkin. Copyright ©1996. Used by permission of Tyndale House Publishers.